To Dan (Super Dan),

Soon to be!
One of the best!!
and not even trying.

All the best

Steve

Brandy Crusta

The Australian Bartender's Guide to Cocktails

Russell Steabben and Frank Corsar

Fourth Edition

HOSPITALITY PRESS
Melbourne

For Gillian Steabben
1955-1989

Hospitality Press Pty Ltd
38 Riddell Parade
P.O. Box 426
Elsternwick Victoria 3185
Australia
Telephone (03) 9528 5021 Fax (03) 9528 2645
email hosppress@access.net.au

The Australian Bartender's Guide to Cocktails

First published 1988
Second edition 1990
Third edition 1994
Fourth edition 1999, reprinted (with corrections) 1999, 2001

National Library of Australia Cataloguing-in-publication data:

Steabben, Russell, 1941– .
  The Australian bartender's guide to cocktails.
4th ed.
Includes index.
ISBN 1 86250 486 5.
1. Cocktails. 2. Bartending - Australia.
I. Corsar, Frank, 1954- . II. Title.

641.8740994

Colour photography by Paul Saville & Associates and Rick de Carteret
Designed and typeset by John van Loon
Production by Publishing Solutions, Richmond, Vic.
Published by Hospitality Press Pty Ltd, Melbourne (ACN 006 473 454)

Contents

Acknowledgements

We have received help from many people in the preparation of this book; too many for us to be able to thank them all. Nevertheless we would particularly like to acknowledge the help of the following people and organizations as without their help this book would not have been possible.

We would like to thank Suntory (Australia) Pty Ltd and Ian Simpson in particular for the photographs of the garnishes and the finished cocktails. We also thank Remy Martin (Australia) Pty Ltd, and Juris Austrums in particular, for the photographs of the glasses and equipment; Coffex Coffee for their contribution to the section on coffee and their support with the photography; George Ellis for allowing us to use two photographs from his *Australian Bar Attendant's Handbook*; Sir Ian and Lady Orton for contributing cocktail recipes and commenting on the draft text; Suntory (Australia) Pty Ltd for suggesting cocktail recipes; David Cunningham of Hospitality Press for his editorial work on the text; the late Gillian Steabben for typing and retyping the text and handling all the time-consuming clerical work involved in the preparation of the original edition; and the branches of the Australian Bartenders Guild in Victoria, South Australia, Western Australia, ACT, North Queensland, South Queensland, and New South Wales for their unflagging support, very many useful suggestions, and for approving and officially endorsing this book.

We would also like to thank the many organizations and individuals who have shared their original creations with us and you. A special thank-you to Mark Filgate for his shooter and recipe advice.

Russell Steabben   Frank Corsar

Introduction

About this book

This book has been written especially for Australian professional bartenders. Because of its step-by-step and informative approach, it has proved immensely useful to both the general public interested in cocktails and to students of Hospitality Studies. It answers all the questions most commonly asked by people first entering the bartending profession and it includes a comprehensive list of recipes for all the cocktails currently in demand in Australian bars.

Why another cocktail book?

We decided that a cocktail book especially for use in Australian bars was needed because all the other many cocktail recipe books which are available were written either for use in other countries or were intended simply for use by amateurs at home. The first edition of *The Australian Bartender's Guide to Cocktails* was the first serious attempt to standardize popular cocktail recipes in Australia. It and the subsequent editions have been fully endorsed by the Australian Bartender's Guild. While most other cocktail books contain large numbers of recipes for cocktails which are very rarely, if ever, mixed in Australian bars, this book concentrates on the recipes in demand today. We pay due respect to the traditional recipes for the classic cocktails, but in Australia variations on some of the traditional recipes are often in demand. In those cases the book gives the recipes both for the traditional cocktail and also for the most popular current Australian variation or variations.

Australian bars vary considerably, of course, and for that reason we have kept the information in the book as general as possible so that it will be suitable for use throughout the country and in bars of all types.

The fourth edition

The fourth edition of *The Australian Bartender's Guide to Cocktails* contains a great many more recipes than the previous edition. Their number has increased by more than fifty per cent. At the same time the less popular recipes which appeared in the third edition have been dropped. Many of the new recipes include a note identifying the establishment where the cocktail originated and/or the name of the bartender who created the drink. Shooters have now established a lasting popularity in this country so recipes for a large number of the best-selling shooters are included in this edition. The fourth edition also includes a new section on coffee and the glossary has been greatly expanded.

We are confident that these improvements will ensure that the fourth edition of *The Australian Bartender's Guide to Cocktails* will retain its popularity as an essential text for hospitality training courses and remain an invaluable reference for the profession and the home library.

The Australian Bartender's Guide to Cocktails is, and should now remain, the book you consistently see being used by working bartenders.

Russell Steabben   Frank Corsar

① The Cocktail

What is a cocktail?

A cocktail is almost impossible to define. It is often described as a mixed drink taken before a meal, a stimulant to the appetite and an aid to digestion. It can be all those things, but it is infinitely more as well.

Most cocktail books imply that cocktails are drinks with a base (usually a spirit like gin or brandy) to which other ingredients are added, but even this wide definition is inadequate. When mixing today's cocktails we often try to achieve a balanced and homogeneous mix of ingredients without there necessarily being a single 'base' to any drink.

Because there are so many conflicting definitions of the cocktail, it is perhaps best to move to a description of the three categories into which modern cocktails fall. There are three internationally recognized styles of cocktail:

> Pre-dinner cocktails
> After-dinner cocktails
> Long drink cocktails.

Pre-dinner cocktails are those acidic or dry drinks mixed using tart ingredients, such as lemon juice, which are intended to refresh the palate and act as an aperitif before a meal.

Drinks made using more creamy ingredients fit into the after-dinner category. They tend to be richer in texture, and they are frequently quite sweet.

The long drink cocktails are those served in a Highball glass, often over ice. They are frequently fruity and are 'softened' with a generous proportion of fruit juices, soft drinks, and milk.

Note however that what matters is not the technical category into which a cocktail falls, or the personal preference of the bartender, but the individual wishes of the customer. The truly professional bartender will always make exactly the style of cocktail the customer wants.

History of the cocktail

The early history of the cocktail is obscure. Several interesting legends about its origin exist but they cannot be substantiated. Even the origin of the word cocktail, which was first used in its present sense in the nineteenth century, is not known. However it is generally accepted that the modern cocktail was first popularized in the USA.

In the early years of the twentieth century cocktails were a feature of life in America among the high-living and wealthy. During the roaring twenties which were the years of Prohibition in America (1919-33), the popularity of cocktails grew rapidly. Although the sale of alcohol was illegal, creative bartenders found ways to camouflage alcoholic drinks with fruit juices and dairy products and so many new cocktails were created and the taste for cocktails spread.

Cocktail parties were a feature of fashionable life in Australia in the thirties but they came to an abrupt end with the onset of World War II. Cocktails did not begin to regain their popularity until the sixties.

Since the mid seventies, with the development of discos and the rebirth of the night club, the market for cocktails has widened to include a much younger public than before. The variety of drinks available today has surpassed all previous eras and there is a trend away from traditional recipes in favour of new and more exciting drinks. With the success of discos and night clubs and films such as *Cocktail* this revived popularity has continued. This trend has been reinforced by the growth in the number of licensed restaurants and by the development of licensed café-bars and bistros all of which stimulate the sales of cocktails.

② The Recipes

To suit all requirements measures for recipes are given in three different ways in this edition of *The Australian Bartender's Guide to Cocktails*. First, exact measures for a single drinks (e.g. 30 mL) are given for each ingredient as we believe this is the most useful way of presenting cocktail recipes. Then the ingredients are given both in parts and in fractions. These follow the ingredient item. The recipe for a Whiskey Sour, for example, is given as:

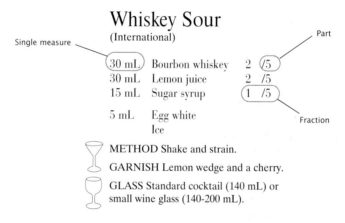

Whiskey Sour
(International)

Single measure — Part

			Fraction
30 mL	Bourbon whiskey	2	/5
30 mL	Lemon juice	2	/5
15 mL	Sugar syrup	1	/5
5 mL	Egg white		
	Ice		

METHOD Shake and strain.

GARNISH Lemon wedge and a cherry.

GLASS Standard cocktail (140 mL) or small wine glass (140-200 mL).

There is a line space between the main ingredients included in the calculation of parts and fractions, and subsidiary ingredients, such as ice or fillers, which have not been included in the calculation of parts and fractions.

The glasses recommended are a guide only; the capacity in millilitres (mL) is usually the key factor, not the shape of the glass.

The recipes recommended by the International Bartenders Association International Cocktail Committee have been followed for the international cocktails (marked 'International'), while the Australian recipes (marked 'Australian') are those recommended by the Australian Bartenders Guild.

After Dinner Mint
(Shooter)
(Australian)

15 mL	Kahlua	1	/3
15 mL	Green crème de menthe	1	/3
15 mL	Bailey's Irish Cream	1	/3

METHOD Layer in the above order.

GARNISH No garnish.

GLASS Shot (60 mL).

Aida's Curse
(Australian)

30 mL	Midori melon liqueur	6	/26
30 mL	Cointreau	6	/26
10 mL	Lena banana liqueur	2	/26
15 mL	Lemon juice	3	/26
45 mL	Pineapple juice	9	/26

Ice

METHOD Shake and strain or build all ingredients except the Lena Banana. Pour Lena down the side of the glass so that it settles at the bottom.

GARNISH No garnish.

GLASS Standard cocktail (140 mL).

Alexander
See Brandy Alexander No 1, No 2 and Midori Alexander.

Amaretto Sour
See Whiskey Sour (note).

Americano
(International)

30 mL	Sweet red vermouth	1	/2
30 mL	Campari	1	/2
	Soda		
	Ice		

METHOD Build over ice. Top up with soda.

GARNISH Half slice of orange and twist of lemon.

GLASS Highball (300 mL).

Anabolic Steroids
(Shooter)

20 mL	Midori melon liqueur	1	/2
20 mL	Triple sec	1	/2

2 drops Blue curaçao

METHOD Layer triple sec over Midori. Add drops of blue curaçao.

GARNISH No garnish.

GLASS Shot (60 mL).

Angel's Tip
(Shooter)
(International)

30 mL	White crème de cacao	3	/4
10 mL	Cream	1	/4

METHOD Layer in the above order.

GARNISH No garnish.

GLASS Shot (60 mL).

Australia III

Angry Fijian
(Shooter)
(Australian)

15 mL Lena banana liqueur   1 /3
15 mL Bailey's Irish Cream   1 /3
15 mL Malibu   1 /3

METHOD Layer in the above order.

GARNISH No garnish.

GLASS Shot (60 mL).

Apotheke
(Pick-me-up)
(International)

20 mL Brandy   4 /10
15 mL Green crème de menthe 3 /10
15 mL Fernet Branca   3 /10

METHOD Stir and strain.

GARNISH No garnish.

GLASS Martini (90 mL).

Apple Breaker
(Mocktail)
(Australian)

60 mL Apple juice
4 drops Angostura bitters

Dry ginger ale
Ice

METHOD Build. Top with ginger ale.

GARNISH Cherry.

GLASS Highball (300 mL).

Apple Delight
(Mocktail)
(Australian)

60 mL Apple juice   4 /8
30 mL Orange juice   2 /8
15 mL Lemon juice   1 /8
15mL   Sugar syrup   1 /8

2 barsp Egg white
Ice

METHOD Blend.

GARNISH Orange and lemon wheels and a cherry.

GLASS Balloon (285 mL).

Apple Jack
(Australian)

30 mL Jack Daniel's whiskey
Apple juice
Ice

METHOD Build whiskey over cubed ice and top with apple juice.

GARNISH Apple or lemon wheel.

GLASS Highball (300 mL).

Arcadia
(Australian)

25 mL Lochan Ora   5 /20
60 mL Sake (hot)   12 /20
15 mL Boiling water   3 /20

METHOD Pour 10 mL of Lochan Ora into the glass. Twirl around. Ignite. Pour in the remaining Lochan Ora, followed by the sake and boiling water.

GARNISH On a garnish plate, half a tinned baby pear, a spiral of orange peel and a piece of ginger, surrounded by a combination of zested lime and lemon peel.

GLASS Standard cocktail (140 mL).

Created by Michael Chapman at Inflation, Melbourne in 1985.

Australia III
(Australian)

30 mL	Midori melon liqueur	2	/4
15 mL	Grand Marnier	1	/4
15 mL	Pineapple juice		
	(unsweetened)	1	/4

1	Egg yolk	
Half	Fresh kiwi fruit	
4 cubes Ice		

METHOD Blend.

GARNISH Kiwi fruit wheel and a cherry.

GLASS Tulip flute (180 mL).

Created by Gillian Steabben at the Australian Catering Academy, 1985.

Australia IV
(Mocktail)
(Australian)

30 mL	Lime green cordial	2	/4
15 mL	Sugar syrup	1	/4
15 mL	Pineapple juice	1	/4

1	Egg yolk
Half	Fresh kiwi fruit
4 cubes Ice	

METHOD Blend.

GARNISH Kiwi fruit wheel with a cherry.

GLASS Standard cocktail (140 mL).

Australian Crawl
(Australian)

15 mL	Dark rum	1	/4
15 mL	Gin	1	/4
15 mL	Vodka	1	/4
15 mL	Scotch whisky	1	/4

Cola
Ice

METHOD Build all ingredients except cola over ice. Top with cola.

GARNISH Lemon wheel.

GLASS Highball (300 mL).

B and B
(International)

30 mL	Bénédictine	1	/2
30 mL	Cognac	1	/2

Ice

METHOD Build into an ice-filled glass.

GARNISH No garnish.

GLASS Balloon (285mL).

B52, No 1
(Short or shooter)
(International)

15 mL	Kahlua	1	/3
15 mL	Bailey's Irish Cream	1	/3
15 mL	Grand Marnier	1	/3

METHOD Layer in the above order.

GARNISH No garnish.

GLASS Shot or port (60 mL).

B52, No 2
(Long)
(Australian)

30 mL	Kahlua	1	/3
30 mL	Bailey's Irish Cream	1	/3
30 mL	Grand Marnier	1	/3

Ice

METHOD Build.

GARNISH Chocolate-dipped strawberry (optional).

 GLASS Balloon (285 mL).

Bacardi Cocktail
(International)

60 mL	Bacardi white rum	2	/3
30 mL	Lemon or lime juice (fresh)	1	/3
5 mL	Grenadine		
5 mL	Egg white		
	Ice		

METHOD Shake and strain.

GARNISH Cherry.

 GLASS Standard cocktail (140 mL).

Banana Bender
(Australian)

30 mL	Lena banana liqueur	1	/4
30 mL	Cointreau	1	/4
30 mL	Pineapple juice (unsweetened)	1	/4
30 mL	Cream	1	/4

2 slices Banana
Half scoop   Ice

METHOD Blend.

GARNISH Banana wheel and a cherry.

GLASS Tulip flute (180 mL).

Banana Colada
(Australian)

30 mL	White rum	1	/7
30 mL	Coconut cream	1	/7
30 mL	Lena banana liqueur	1	/7
90 mL	Pineapple juice	3	/7
30 mL	Cream	1	/7

Half   Large banana
1 scoop Ice

METHOD Place all ingredients into blender and blend for about ten seconds.

GARNISH Slice of banana and a cherry.

GLASS Colada (400 mL).

Banana Daiquiri
(International)

30 mL	White rum	6	/10
15 mL	Crème de banane or Lena banana liqueur	3	/10
5 mL	Lemon or lime juice	1	/10

Half   Small banana
1 scoop Crushed ice

METHOD Blend at high speed. Pour into glass without straining.

GARNISH Banana wheel and a cherry.

GLASS Tulip flute (180 mL).

Banana Fizz
(Australian)

30 mL	Lena banana liqueur	2	/5
30 mL	Lemon juice	2	/5
15 mL	Sugar syrup	1	/5

1   Egg white
Half   Banana
        Soda
        Ice

METHOD Blend all ingredients except soda. Top with soda.

GARNISH Banana wheel and a cherry.

GLASS Highball (300 mL).

Banana Margarita
(Australian)

30 mL	Tequila	2	/6
15 mL	Cointreau	1	/6
15 mL	Lena banana liqueur	1	/6
30 mL	Lemon juice	2	/6

5 mL	Egg white (optional)
Half	Small banana
	Ice

METHOD Blend.

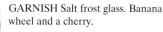 GARNISH Salt frost glass. Banana wheel and a cherry.

GLASS Tulip flute (180 mL).

Banana Mender
(Mocktail)
(Australian)

30 mL	Sugar syrup	2	/8
45 mL	Pineapple juice	3	/8
45 mL	Cream	3	/8

Half	Small banana
Half scoop	Ice

METHOD Blend.

GARNISH Banana wheel or a cherry.

GLASS Tulip flute (180 mL).

Bananarama
(Australian)

30 mL	Kahlua	2	/4
15 mL	Bailey's Irish Cream	1	/4
15 mL	Lena banana liqueur	1	/4

One-third   Fresh banana
75 mL   Cream
1 sm. scoop   Ice

METHOD Blend.

 GARNISH Dribble chocolate topping down the glass to create a swirl effect before adding the drink to the glass. Strawberry and chocolate flake garnish on top of the drink.

GLASS Colada (400 mL).

From the Crown Entertainment Complex, Melbourne.

Banshee
(Australian)

30 mL	Lena banana liqueur	1	/4
30 mL	White crème de cacao	1	/4
60 mL	Cream	2	/4

Ice

METHOD Shake and strain.

 GARNISH Cherry.

GLASS Standard cocktail (140 mL).

Beaufort Connection
(Australian)

30 mL	Orange curaçao	2	/11
30 mL	Galliano	2	/11
30 mL	Lemon juice	2	/11
30 mL	Pineapple juice	2	/11
45 mL	Orange juice	3	/11

Ice

METHOD Shake and strain.

GARNISH Orange wedge.

GLASS Champagne saucer.

From the Mezzanine Lounge Bar, The Heritage, Brisbane.

Bee Sting
(Mocktail)
(Australian)

90 mL	Apple juice	6	/9
30 mL	Orange Juice	2	/9
15 mL	Lime juice	1	/9

2 barsp Honey
Ice

METHOD Build.

 GARNISH Orange wheel.

GLASS Old Fashioned (180-240 mL).

Beetlejuice

(Shooter)
(Australian)

20 mL	Midori melon liqueur	2	/9
20 mL	Amaretto	2	/9
20 mL	Absolut vodka	2	/9
30 mL	Cranberry juice	3	/9

METHOD Layer in the above order.

GARNISH No garnish.

GLASS Shot (90 mL).

From Planet Hollywood, Sydney.

Bellini

(International)

45 mL	Peach juice (nectar)	1	/3
90 mL	Sparkling wine (méthode champenoise)	2	/3

METHOD Build peach juice. Top with sparkling wine.

GARNISH None.

GLASS Tulip flute (180 mL).

Better than Sex

(Australian)

30 mL	White sambuca	2	/10
15 mL	Kahlua	1	/10
60 mL	Milk	4	/10
30 mL	Cream	2	/10
15 mL	Opal Nera	1	/10

1 scoop Ice cream
Ice

METHOD Blend all ingredients except Opal Nera. Pour Opal Nera on top.

GARNISH Cherry, strawberry and plastic animal.

GLASS Colada (400 mL).

From Grumpy's Restaurant, Main Beach, Gold Coast, Queensland.

Between the Sheets

(International)

30 mL	Brandy	2	/7
30 mL	White rum	2	/7
30 mL	Cointreau	2	/7
15 mL	Lemon juice	1	/7

Ice

METHOD Shake and strain.

GARNISH Spiral of orange peel (optional).

GLASS Standard cocktail (140 mL).

Bitter Apples

(Mocktail)
(Australian)

15 mL Lime cordial
6 drops Angostura bitters
Apple juice
Ice

METHOD Build. Top with apple juice.

GARNISH Lemon or orange wheel and a cherry.

GLASS Highball (300 mL).

Bitter Lime

(Mocktail)
(Australian)

30 mL Lime cordial
Bitter lemon
Ice

METHOD Build. Top with bitter lemon.

GARNISH Lemon wheel.

GLASS Highball (300 mL).

Black and Tan

See glossary

Black and Tan

(Mocktail)
(Australian)

Cola
Milk
Ice

METHOD Place the ice in the glass and fill the glass two-thirds full of cola. Top with milk.

GARNISH Strawberry.

GLASS Highball (300 mL).

Black Jellybean

See Jellybean (note).

Black Magic

(Australian)

30 mL	Jamaica rum	2	/10
15 mL	Kahlua	1	/10
30 mL	Suntory mango liqueur	2	/10
30 mL	Orange juice	2	/10
30 mL	Pineapple juice (unsweetened)	2	/10
15 mL	Lemon juice	1	/10

2 slices Mango
1 scoop Ice

METHOD Blend.

GARNISH Black straws.

GLASS Balloon (285 mL).

Black Nipple

(Shooter)
(Australian)

15 mL	Opal Nera	1	/2
15 mL	Bailey's Irish Cream	1	/2

METHOD Layer in the above order.

GARNISH No garnish.

GLASS Shot (60 mL).

Black Nuts, No 1

(Australian)

30 mL	Frangelico	1	/2
30 mL	Opal Nera	1	/2

Crushed ice

METHOD Build.

GARNISH Strawberry.

GLASS Martini (90 mL).

Black Nuts, No 2

(Shooter)
(Australian)

30 mL	Frangelico	1	/2
30 mL	Opal Nera	1	/2

METHOD Layer in the above order.

GARNISH No garnish.

GLASS Shot (60 mL).

Black Russian, No 1
(International)

30 mL	Vodka	2	/3
15 mL	Kahlua	1	/3
	Ice		

METHOD Build into an ice-filled Old Fashioned glass.

GARNISH No garnish.

GLASS Old Fashioned (180-240 mL).

Black Russian, No 2
(Short)
(Australian)

30 mL	Vodka	1	/2
30 mL	Kahlua	1	/2
	Ice		

METHOD Build into an ice-filled Old Fashioned glass.

GARNISH No garnish.

GLASS Old Fashioned (180-240 mL).

NOTE The Australian Black Russian has a higher proportion of Kahlua in relation to vodka than the standard international drink. Many Australian bars substitute Tia Maria or dark crème de cacao for Kahlua.

Black Russian, No 3
(Long)
(Australian)

30 mL	Vodka	1	/2
30 mL	Kahlua	1	/2
	Cola		
	Ice		

METHOD Build vodka and Kahlua over ice in a Highball glass. Top with cola. Stir gently.

GARNISH No garnish.

GLASS Highball (300 mL).

Black Velvet
(Champagne cocktail)
(International)

| Half | Guinness stout (chilled) | 1 | /2 |
| Half | Sparkling wine (méthode champenoise) | 1 | /2 |

METHOD Half fill a conical pilsner glass with chilled sparkling wine, taking care not to lose much of the sparkle (gas). Carefully pour the Guinness on top. Great care must be taken as the drink can foam uncontrollably if it is poured carelessly.

GARNISH No garnish.

GLASS Conical pilsner.

Black Widow
(Shooter)
(Australian)

15 mL	Strawberry liqueur	1	/3
15 mL	Opal Nera	1	/3
15 mL	Cream	1	/3

METHOD Layer in the above order.

GARNISH No garnish.

GLASS Shot (60 mL).

Bloodbath
(Shooter)
(Australian)

| 30 mL | Tequila | 1 | /2 |
| 30 mL | Suntory strawberry liqueur | 1 | /2 |

METHOD Layer in the above order.

GARNISH No garnish.

GLASS Shot (60 mL).

Bloody Mary

Bloody Lovely
(Australian)

30 mL	Midori melon liqueur	1	/4
30 mL	Bailey's Irish Cream	1	/4
30 mL	Malibu	1	/4
30 mL	Cream	1	/4
4	Strawberries (fresh)		
	Ice		

METHOD Blend.

GARNISH Half strawberry.

GLASS Balloon (285 mL).

Bloody Mary
(Australian version)

30 mL	Vodka	2	/13
150 mL	Tomato juice	10	/13
15 mL	Lemon juice	1	/13
2 drops	Tabasco		
5-10 mL	Worcestershire sauce		
	Salt and pepper (to taste)		
	Ice		

METHOD Build all ingredients except tomato juice into a Highball glass half-filled with ice. Top with tomato juice and stir thoroughly.

GARNISH Slice of lemon, stick of celery, two straws.

GLASS Highball (300 mL).

NOTE The same drink without the vodka is called a Virgin Mary.

Blow Job
(Shooter)
(Australian)

15 mL	Kahlua	1	/4
15 mL	Bailey's Irish Cream	1	/4
15 mL	Lena banana liqueur	1	/4
15 mL	Cream	1	/4

METHOD Layer in the above order.

GARNISH No garnish.

GLASS Shot (60 mL).

Blueberry Delight
(Australian)

20 mL	Opal Nera	1	/6
20 mL	Suntory strawberry liqueur	1	/6
20 mL	Malibu	1	/6
60 mL	Cream	3	/6
	Ice		

METHOD Shake and strain.

GARNISH No garnish.

GLASS Standard cocktail (140 mL).

Blue Hawaii
(Australian)

30 mL	Bacardi white rum	2	/6
15 mL	Blue curaçao	1	/6
15 mL	Cointreau	1	/6
30 mL	Cream	2	/6
	Ice		

METHOD Shake and strain.

GARNISH Cherry.

GLASS Standard cocktail (140 mL).

Blue Lady
(International)

30 mL	Gin	2	/4
15 mL	Blue curaçao	1	/4
15 mL	Lemon juice	1	/4
5 mL	Egg white (optional)		
	Ice		

METHOD Shake and strain.

GARNISH Cherry.

GLASS Martini (90 mL).

Blue Lagoon, No 1
(International)

30 mL	Vodka	6	/10
5 mL	Blue curaçao	1	/10
15 mL	Lemon juice	3	/10
	Ice		

METHOD Shake and strain.

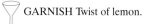 GARNISH Twist of lemon.

GLASS Standard cocktail (140 mL).

Blue Lagoon, No 2
(Australian)

30 mL	Vodka	2	/3
15 mL	Blue curaçao	1	/3
	Lemonade		
	Ice		

METHOD Half fill a Highball glass with ice. Pour vodka and curaçao over ice and top with lemonade.

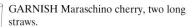 GARNISH Maraschino cherry, two long straws.

GLASS Highball (300 mL).

Blue Negligée
(Australian)

20 mL	Green Chartreuse	1	/3
20 mL	Parfait Amour	1	/3
20 mL	Ouzo	1	/3
	Ice		

METHOD Stir and strain.

GARNISH No garnish.

GLASS Martini (90 mL).

Created by Frank Clark. Winner of the ABG National Competition, 1965.

Boilermaker
(International)

30 mL	Scotch whisky
	Beer

A Boilermaker is a whisky with a beer chaser (served in separate glasses).

Bosom Caresser
(International)

30 mL	Brandy	6	/10
15 mL	Orange curaçao	3	/10
5 mL	Grenadine	1	/10
1	Egg yolk		
	Ice		

METHOD Shake and strain.

 GARNISH Cherry.

GLASS Standard cocktail (140 mL).

Brandy Alexander, No 1
(International)

15 mL	Brandy	1	/3
15 mL	Brown crème de cacao	1	/3
15 mL	Cream	1	/3
	Ice		

METHOD Shake and strain.

GARNISH Grated nutmeg (a light sprinkle).

GLASS Martini (90 mL).

NOTE The trend in Australia with this, as with most cream cocktails, is to increase the proportion of cream. It is now common to present cream cocktails in a standard cocktail glass (140 mL) instead of the traditional Martini glass (90 mL) because the larger glass allows more cream to be included. See next recipe.

Brandy Alexander, No 2
(Australian)

30 mL	Brandy	1	/4
30 mL	Brown crème de cacao	1	/4
60 mL	Cream	2	/4
	Ice		

METHOD Shake and strain.

GARNISH Grated nutmeg (a light sprinkle), maraschino cherry (optional).

GLASS Standard cocktail (140 mL).

Brandy Crusta
(Australian)

30 mL	Brandy	2	/9
30 mL	Sweet vermouth	2	/9
15 mL	Maraschino	1	/9
60 mL	Orange juice (processed)	4	/9

2 drops Angostura bitters
Ice

METHOD Shake and strain.

GARNISH Sugar-frosted glass. Orange spiral (optional).

GLASS Large champagne saucer or wine glass (180 mL).

NOTE Use processed orange juice, that is tinned or packaged. It has a thicker consistency, stronger flavour, and richer colour than fresh orange juice.

Brandy Egg-nog
(International)

30 mL	Brandy	6	/7
5 mL	Sugar syrup	1	/7
1	Egg yolk		
	Milk		

METHOD Shake and strain all ingredients except milk into glass. Top with milk.

GARNISH Grated nutmeg.

GLASS Highball (300 mL).

Brandy, Lime, and Soda
(International)

30 mL	Brandy	2	/3
15 mL	Lime cordial	1	/3
	Soda		
	Ice		

METHOD Half fill a Highball glass with ice. Add the brandy. Top with soda (leaving room for the lime). Add lime cordial. Stir.

GARNISH Slice of lemon. Two straws.

GLASS Highball (300 mL).

NOTE Extra lime cordial can be added for those with a sweeter palate. The lime cordial's consistency is heavier than the soda's. Adding the cordial last minimises mixing and reduces the loss of sparkle from the soda. Premium quality soda should be used for the best results.

Brandy Sour
See Whiskey Sour (note).

Brandy Alexander

Bronx

(International)

30 mL	Gin	2	/5
15 mL	Dry vermouth	1	/5
15 mL	Sweet red vermouth	1	/5
15 mL	Orange juice	1	/5
	Ice		

METHOD Shake and strain.

GARNISH Strawberry.

GLASS Martini (90 mL).

Brown Cow

(Australian)

30 mL	Kahlua
	Milk
	Ice

METHOD Half fill a Highball glass with ice. Add the Kahlua, top with milk, stir.

GARNISH Long straws.

GLASS Highball (300 mL).

Bubble Gum

(Australian)

30 mL	Malibu	1	/4
30 mL	Galliano	1	/4
60 mL	Cream	2	/4
5 mL	Grenadine		
	Ice		

METHOD Shake and strain.

GARNISH Cherry.

GLASS Standard cocktail (140 mL).

Buck's Fizz (Mimosa)

(Champagne cocktail)
(International)

90 mL	Sparkling wine (iced)	3	/5
60 mL	Orange juice	2	/5

METHOD Build fresh orange juice. Top with iced sparkling wine.

GARNISH Lemon spiral (optional).

GLASS Saucer or flute (180 mL).

NOTE A Buck's Fizz is also known as a Mimosa.

Buck's Fizzer

(Mocktail)
(Australian)

30 mL	Lime cordial
	Orange juice (chilled)
	Mineral water

METHOD Place the lime cordial in the glass and top with half chilled orange juice and half mineral water.

GARNISH Half orange wheel.

GLASS Flute (180 mL).

Bullshot

(International)

30 mL	Vodka	3	/10
60 mL	Beef bouillon (or condensed consommé)	6	/10
10 mL	Lemon juice	1	/10
10 mL	Worcestershire sauce		
5 mL	Tabasco		
	Salt		
	Pepper		
	Celery salt		
	Ice		

METHOD Build over ice in glass. Stir.

GARNISH Slice of lemon.

GLASS Highball (300 mL).

Bush Oyster

See Prairie Oyster (note).

Campari and Soda

(International)

30 mL Campari
        Soda
        Ice

METHOD Half fill the glass with ice,
add the Campari and top with soda.

GARNISH Half slice of lemon.

GLASS Old Fashioned (180-240 mL).

Casanova

(Mocktail)
(Australian)

20 mL	Monin yellow banana	2	/18
30 mL	Monin coconut	3	/18
100 mL	Pineapple juice	10	/18
30 mL	Cream	3	/18

Quarter Fresh banana
        Ice

METHOD Blend.

GARNISH Pineapple wedge and a
cherry.

GLASS Wine glass (240 mL).

Champagne Cocktail

(International)

15 mL Brandy
1   Sugar cube
4 drops Angostura bitters
        Sparkling wine
        (méthode champenoise)

METHOD Pour the Angostura bitters
over the sugar cube. Place it in the glass.
Add the brandy. Fill the glass with chilled
sparkling wine.

GARNISH Half slice of orange.

GLASS Saucer or flute (180 mL).

VARIATIONS Cointreau or Grand
Marnier are sometimes used instead of
brandy (or cognac). A combination of
cognac and Cointreau is another possible
substitute for brandy. A thin spiral of
orange peel can be used as an alternative
garnish.

Champagne Mocktail

(Australian)

| 60 mL | Apple juice | 2 | /3 |
| 30 mL | Lemon cordial | 1 | /3 |

        Mineral water
4 drops Angostura bitters
        Sugar cube

METHOD Build.

GARNISH Angostura bitters on the sugar
cube.

GLASS Flute (180 mL).

Champagne Pick-me-up
(International)

30 mL	Brandy	1	/2
30 mL	Orange juice	1	/2
5 mL	Grenadine		
	Sparkling wine		
	(méthode champenoise)		
	Ice		

METHOD Shake and strain brandy, orange juice, and grenadine into glass. Top with chilled sparkling wine.

GARNISH No garnish.

GLASS Flute (180 mL).

Champagne Strawberry Punch
(Australian)

180 mL	Suntory strawberry liqueur	
2 bottles	Sparkling wine	
	(méthode champenoise)	
2 punnets	Strawberries	
	Icing sugar	
	Ice	

METHOD Clean strawberries and slice them in half. Use enough icing sugar to coat the strawberries thoroughly. Add strawberry liqueur and stir. Refrigerate overnight. Place mixture in a punch bowl and pour sparkling wine carefully over it. Lightly mix. When serving ensure each serve contains some of the strawberry mixture. For the best results serve immediately.

GLASS Champagne saucer.

SERVES Fifteen.

Chastity Belt
(Shooter)
(Australian)

15 mL	Tia Maria	1	/4
15 mL	Frangelico	1	/4
15 mL	Bailey's Irish Cream	1	/4
15 mL	Cream	1	/4

METHOD Layer in the above order.

GARNISH No garnish.

GLASS Shot (60 mL).

Cherry Alexander
(Australian)

30 mL	Cherry brandy	1	/4
30 mL	Brown crème de cacao	1	/4
60 mL	Cream	2	/4
	Ice		

METHOD Shake and strain.

GARNISH Two cherries.

GLASS Standard cocktail (140 mL).

Cherry Ripe
(Australian)

30 mL	Cherry brandy	1	/5
30 mL	Malibu	1	/5
30 mL	Tia Maria	1	/5
60 mL	Cream	2	/5
4	Dark cherries		
	Ice		

METHOD Blend.

GARNISH A piece of Cherry Ripe.

GLASS Colada (400 mL).

Chi Chi
(International)

45 mL	Vodka	3	/13
30 mL	Coconut cream	2	/13
120 mL	Pineapple juice		
	(unsweetened)	8	/13

2 scoops Ice

METHOD Blend.

GARNISH Pineapple stick, cherry.

GLASS Colada (400 mL).

Chocolate Eclair
(Australian)

30 mL	Cadbury's Cream		
	Liqueur	1	/4
30 mL	Kahlua	1	/4
60 mL	Cream	2	/4

Ice

METHOD Shake and strain.

GARNISH Strawberry and flake chocolate.

GLASS Standard cocktail (140 mL).

Chocolate Sailor
See Siggi's Chocolate Sailor.

Cinderella
(Mocktail)
(International)

60 mL	Lemon juice	1	/3
60 mL	Orange juice	1	/3
60 mL	Pineapple juice		
	(unsweetened)	1	/3

Ice

METHOD Shake and strain.

GARNISH Whole orange slice on the side of the glass, half slice of lemon, and pineapple wedge.

GLASS Old Fashioned (180-240 mL).

Citrus Sombrero
(Australian)

30 mL	Dry vermouth	6	/14
10 mL	Campari	2	/14
15 mL	Monin ginger syrup	3	/14
15 mL	Monin mandarin syrup	3	/14

Soda
Ice

METHOD Build. Top with soda.

GARNISH Orange wheel and a cherry.

GLASS Flute (180 ml).

From Prosser's on the Beach Restaurant, Sandy Bay, Hobart.

Clayton's
(Mocktail)
(Australian)

30 mL	Clayton's
	Dry ginger ale
	Lemonade
	Ice

METHOD Pour Clayton's over ice. Top up with equal parts of dry ginger ale and lemonade.

GARNISH Slice of lemon.

GLASS Highball (300 mL).

Cointreau Frappé
(International)

30 mL Cointreau
       Crushed ice

METHOD Fill glass with crushed ice.
Build Cointreau over. (See Frappés.)

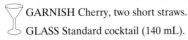 GARNISH Cherry, two short straws.

GLASS Standard cocktail (140 mL).

Coladas
See Banana Colada, Mango Colada,
Midori Colada, Pina Coladas, and
Strawberry Coladas.

Collins
See Tom Collins.

Collins Mocktail
(Australian)

30 mL Lemon juice   1   /2
30 mL Sugar syrup   1   /2

4 drops Angostura bitters
        Soda
        Ice

METHOD Build. Top with soda.

GARNISH Lemon wheel.

GLASS Highball (300 mL).

Comfortable Screw
(International)

30 mL Vodka   2   /3
15 mL Southern Comfort   1   /3
       Orange juice
       Ice

METHOD Build vodka and Southern
Comfort. Top with orange juice.

GARNISH Orange wheel and a cherry.

GLASS Highball (300 mL).

See also Long Sloe Comfortable Screw
up against the Wall and Sloe
Comfortable Screw.

Cool Lemon
(Mocktail)
(Australian)

30 mL Lemon juice   1   /5
30 mL Sugar syrup   1   /5
90 mL Milk   3   /5

       Ice

METHOD Shake and strain.

GARNISH Strawberry.

GLASS Tulip flute (180 mL).

Corpse Reviver
(Pick-me-up)
(Australian)

30 mL Brandy   2   /4
15 mL Calvados   1   /4
15 mL Sweet vermouth   1   /4

       Ice

METHOD Stir and strain.

GARNISH Twist of lemon.

GLASS Martini (90 mL).

Crème de Menthe Frappé

Cowboy

See C.S. Cowboy (below).

Crème de Menthe Frappé

(International)

30 mL   Crème de menthe
        Crushed ice

METHOD Fill glass with crushed ice. Build crème de menthe over. (See Frappés.)

GARNISH Cherry.

GLASS Standard cocktail (140 mL).

Crusta

(Mocktail)
(Australian)

15 mL   Sugar syrup   1 /7
30 mL   Cherry syrup   2 /7
60 mL   Orange juice   4 /7

2 drops Angostura bitters
        Ice

METHOD Shake and strain.

GARNISH Sugar-frosted glass and a cherry.

GLASS Champagne saucer.

C.S.Cowboy

(Shooter)
(Australian)

30 mL   Butterscotch schnapps   2/3
15 mL   Bailey's Irish Cream   1/3

METHOD Layer in the above order.

GARNISH No garnish.

GLASS Shot (60 mL).

Cuba Libre

(International)

45 mL   White rum   3 /4
15 mL   Lime juice (fresh) 1 /4

3 drops Angostura bitters
        Cola
        Ice

METHOD Half fill the glass with ice, add rum and Angostura bitters. Squeeze the juice of the lime into the drink, and drop in the spent shell. Top with cola.

GARNISH One spent lime shell, as above.

GLASS Highball (300 mL).

Daiquiri

(International)

60 mL   White rum   6 /10
30 mL   Lemon or lime juice
        (fresh)   3 /10
10 mL   Sugar syrup   1 /10

        Ice

METHOD Shake and strain.

GARNISH Cherry.

GLASS Standard cocktail (140 mL).

NOTE This recipe is used all round the world, but the proportions vary considerably from place to place. Some bartenders use more or less sugar syrup than others so altering the sweetness of the drink. As fresh limes are relatively expensive and often difficult to obtain, fresh lemon juice is frequently substituted. Egg white is often used in order to improve the appearance of the drink.

Daiquiri, Frozen
(International)

60 mL White rum	6	/10
30 mL Lemon or lime juice		
(fresh)	3	/10
10 mL Sugar syrup	1	/10

1 scoopIce (very small cubes
   or crushed)

METHOD Blend.

GARNISH Cherry.

GLASS Champagne saucer.

NOTE The Frozen Daiquiri is mixed in a blender. If the proportions of ice and ingredients are mixed correctly the finished product will resemble shaved ice. For the best results all ingredients, including the glass, should be refrigerated, or kept in the freezer. In order to obtain the desired frozen appearance and consistency, equal proportions of ice and ingredients should be used. The blender should be on slow speed for about ten seconds.

Daiquiri, Fruit
See Fruit Daiquiri and Strawberry Daiquiri (note).

Death by Choctail
(Australian)

30 mL Bailey's Irish Cream	1	/3
30 mL Chocolate liqueur	1	/3
30 mL Cream	1	/3

Quarter Banana
Ice

METHOD Blend.

GARNISH Chocolate flakes.

GLASS Standard cocktail (140 mL).

From the Birdcage Bar, Wrest Point Casino, Hobart.

Death in the Afternoon
(Champagne cocktail)
(Australian)

15 mL Pernod
   Sparkling wine
   (méthode champenoise)
   Sugar cube

METHOD Place sugar cube in glass, add Pernod, top with sparkling wine.

GARNISH No garnish.

GLASS Tulip flute (180 mL).

Dirty Mother
(Australian)

30 mL Tequila	1	/3
30 mL Grand Marnier	1	/3
30 mL Kahlua	1	/3

Milk
Ice

METHOD Half fill the glass with ice. Add Tequila, Grand Marnier, and Kahlua. Top with milk.

GARNISH Cherry.

GLASS Highball (300 mL).

Dizzy Dame
(International)

30 mL Brandy	2	/6
15 mL Kahlua	1	/6
15 mL Cherry brandy	1	/6
30 mL Cream	2	/6

Ice

METHOD Blend.

GARNISH Slice of orange and a cherry.

GLASS Tulip flute (180 mL).

D.O.A. (Dead on Arrival)
(Shooter)
(Australian)

15 mL	Frangelico	1	/4
15 mL	Peach liqueur	1	/4
15 mL	Brown crème de cacao	1	/4
15 mL	Bailey's Irish Cream	1	/4

METHOD Layer in the above order.

GARNISH No garnish.

GLASS Shot (60 mL).

Dorothy Lamour
(Australian)

30 mL	White rum	2	/5
30 mL	Lena banana liqueur	2	/5
15 mL	Lemon juice	1	/5

3 slices Mango
1 scoop Ice

METHOD Blend.

GARNISH Banana wheel and a cherry.

GLASS Tulip flute (180 mL).

Dr Pepper
See Glossary.

Drought Breaker
(Mocktail)
(Australian)

30 mL Lime cordial
4 drops Angostura bitters
Dry ginger ale
Ice

METHOD Half fill the glass with ice. Add bitters, dry ginger ale and, last, the lime cordial.

GARNISH Two half lemon slices in the drink. One whole lemon slice on the rim of the glass. Straws.

GLASS Highball (300 mL).

Dry Manhattan
See Manhattan, Dry.

Dry Martini
See Martini, Dry.

Face Sucker
(Shooter)
(Australian)

20 mL	Midori melon liqueur	1	/3
20 mL	Mandarine Napoléon	1	/3
20 mL	Cream	1	/3

METHOD Layer in the above order.

GARNISH No garnish.

GLASS Shot (60 mL).

Fatal Attraction
(Australian)

30 mL	Southern Comfort	2	/8
30 mL	Peach liqueur	2	/8
15 mL	Galliano	1	/8
15 mL	Orange juice	1	/8
30 mL	Cream	2	/8

Ice

METHOD Shake and strain.

GARNISH Cherry.

GLASS Standard cocktail (140 mL).

Fizzes
See Gin Fizz and note and particular fizzes as listed under 'FIZZES' in index.

Flaming Lamborghini, No 1
(Australian)

30 mL	Kahlua	2	/5
30 mL	Sambuca	2	/5
15 mL	Cream	1	/5

Nutmeg

METHOD Pour the Kahlua into the glass, then layer the Sambuca on top, pouring it over the back of a barspoon. Ignite the liqueurs, then sprinkle a small quantity of nutmeg on them. This will produce sparks. After a few seconds spoon the cream on top.

GARNISH Grated chocolate, two short straws (optional).

 GLASS Martini (90 mL).

NOTE It is much easier to set the liqueurs alight if they and/or the glass are warmed before you start mixing. There are many variations on the recipe for a Lamborghini. This one and the variation below are the two most common.

Flaming Lamborghini, No 2
(Variation)

20 mL	Kahlua	1	/4
20 mL	Cointreau	1	/4
20 mL	Sambuca	1	/4
20 mL	Cream	1	/4

METHOD Warm ingredients except cream. Pour into glass. Ignite with a match. Extinguish the flame by pouring cream on top.

 GARNISH Grated chocolate.

GLASS Standard cocktail (140 mL)

Florida
(Mocktail)
(International)

60 mL	Grape juice	2	/5
30 mL	Orange juice	1	/5
30 mL	Lemon juice	1	/5
30 mL	Sugar syrup	1	/5

Soda
Ice

METHOD Shake and strain into a glass half-filled with ice. Top with soda.

GARNISH Fruits in season. Long straws.

GLASS Large Highball (400 mL).

Fluffy Duck, No 1
(Australian)

30 mL	Advocaat	2	/7
30 mL	Gin	2	/7
15 mL	Cointreau	1	/7
30 mL	Orange juice	2	/7

Soda
Ice

METHOD Pour approximately 60 mL of soda into the glass. Add advocaat. Mix thoroughly with a bar spoon. Add half a scoop of ice, gin, Cointreau, orange juice, and stir. Top with soda.

GARNISH Long straws, orange wheel and a cherry.

GLASS Highball (300 mL).

NOTE There seem to be as many recipes for this drink as there are bars. However this is the original recipe, which won an Australian cocktail competition in 1963. When mixing a Fluffy Duck it is essential that the advocaat is thoroughly blended into the drink. Avoid where possible using a measure for the advocaat; free pour instead. If you use a measure there is a risk that the measure will develop a nasty smell.

Fluffy Duck, No 2
(Australian)

30 mL	Advocaat	2	/9
30 mL	Gin	2	/9
15 mL	Cointreau	1	/9
30 mL	Orange juice	2	/9
30 mL	Cream	2	/9
	Lemonade		
	Ice		

METHOD Pour about 60 mL of lemonade into the glass. Add advocaat. Mix thoroughly with a bar spoon. Add half a scoop of ice, gin, Cointreau, and orange juice. Stir. Top with lemonade.

GARNISH Orange wheel and a cherry. Long straws.

GLASS Highball (300 mL).

Fluffy Duck Mocktail
(Australian)

15 mL	Sugar syrup	1	/5
30 mL	Orange juice	2	/5
30 mL	Cream	2	/5
1	Egg yolk		
	Lemonade		
	Ice		

METHOD Pour 60 mL of lemonade into glass, add egg yolk and mix thoroughly with a bar spoon. Add ice, sugar syrup, orange juice and cream. Stir with bar spoon. Top with lemonade.

GARNISH Orange wheel and a cherry.

GLASS Highball (300 mL).

Flying Kangaroo
(Australian)

30 mL	Vodka	6	/35
30 mL	Mount Gay rum	6	/35
10 mL	Galliano	2	/35
20 mL	Cream	4	/35
45 mL	Pineapple juice	9	/35
20 mL	Coconut cream	4	/35
20 mL	Orange juice	4	/35
	Ice		

METHOD Blend.

GARNISH Pineapple wedge.

GLASS Colada (400 mL).

Fokker Friendship
(Shooter)
(Australian)

15 mL	Crème de cassis	1	/3
15 mL	Crème de Grand Marnier	1	/3
15 mL	Peachtree liqueur	1	/3

METHOD Layer in the above order.

GARNISH No garnish.

GLASS Shot (60 mL).

Frappés

To make a Frappé, slightly overfill a cocktail glass with finely crushed ice. (*Frappé* is French for crushed or beaten.) Pour a measure (30 mL) of any liqueur or blend of liqueurs over the ice. Garnish with a cherry and two short straws. See Cointreau Frappé, Crème de Menthe Frappé, and Midori-and-Cointreau Frappé.

Freddy Fudpucker
(Australian)

30 mL	Tequila	2	/3
15 mL	Galliano	1	/3

Orange juice
Ice

METHOD Fill the glass with ice. Pour the tequila and orange juice over ice. Float the Galliano on top.

GARNISH Half slice of orange and a cherry.

GLASS Highball (300 mL).

French Connection
(International)

30 mL	Brandy	1	/2
30 mL	Amaretto di Saronno	1	/2

Ice

METHOD Build over ice.

GARNISH No garnish.

GLASS Old Fashioned (180-240 mL).

French 75
(Champagne cocktail)
(International)

30 mL	Gin	2	/5
30 mL	Lemon juice (fresh)	2	/5
15 mL	Sugar syrup	1	/5

Sparkling wine
(méthode champenoise)
Ice

METHOD Shake and strain the gin, lemon juice and sugar syrup. Strain into a Highball glass. Add a few cubes of ice. Top with sparkling wine.

GARNISH No garnish.

GLASS Highball (300 mL).

NOTE Pour carefully so as not to lose too much sparkle.

Frozen Daiquiri
See Daiquiri, Frozen.

Frozen Leango
(Australian)

30 mL	Gin	1	/5
30 mL	Lena banana liqueur	1	/5
30 mL	Mango liqueur	1	/5
60 mL	Orange juice	2	/5

2 scoops   Ice

METHOD Blend.

GARNISH Two long black straws.

GLASS Colada (400 mL).

Created by Graham Brown. Winner of the Suntory Cocktail Competition, 1989.

Frozen Margarita
See Margarita, Frozen.

Fruit Daiquiri
See Strawberry Daiquiri (note), also Banana Daiquiri, Peach Daiquiri, Poached Pear and Ginger Daiquiri.

Fruit Tingle
(Australian)

15 mL	Vodka	1	/2
15 mL	Blue curaçao	1	/2

5 mL	Raspberry cordial
	Lemonade
	Ice

METHOD Build the ice, blue curaçao and vodka. Top with lemonade. Add raspberry cordial.

GARNISH No garnish.

GLASS Highball (300 mL).

Full House

(Australian)

15 mL	Coruba rum	1	/4
30 mL	Kahlua	2	/4
15 mL	Lena banana liqueur	1	/4

Half	Banana
5 mL	Milk
5 mL	Cream
	Ice

METHOD Blend.

GARNISH Strawberry.

GLASS Colada (400 mL).

From the Lobby Bar, The Reef Hotel Casino, Cairns, Queensland.

Galliano Hot Shot

(Shooter)
(Australian)

20 mL	Galliano	1	/3
20 mL	Hot coffee	1	/3
20 mL	Cream, lightly thickened	1	/3

METHOD Layer in the above order.

GARNISH No garnish.

GLASS Shot (60 mL).

Garibaldi

(International)

45 mL	Campari
	Orange juice
	Ice

METHOD Build Campari over ice. Top with orange juice.

GARNISH Half slice of orange (optional).

GLASS Highball (300 mL).

Gibson

(Martini variation)
(International)

| 60 mL | Gin | 9 | /10 |
| 5 mL | Dry vermouth | 1 | /10 |

Ice (cubed or cracked)

METHOD Stir and strain. Fill a mixing glass two-thirds full with cubed or cracked ice. Pour in the ingredients. Stir gently until the ingredients are cold (about ten seconds). Strain into a chilled cocktail glass.

GARNISH A pearl (white) cocktail onion.

GLASS Martini (90 mL).

Gimlet

(International)

| 60 mL | Gin (or vodka) | 2 | /3 |
| 30 mL | Lime juice cordial | 1 | /3 |

Ice

METHOD Shake and strain.

GARNISH No garnish.

GLASS Standard cocktail (140 mL).

Gin-and-French

(Martini variation)
(International)

| 30 mL | Dry 'French' vermouth | 2 | /5 |
| 45 mL | Gin (London dry) | 3 | /5 |

Ice

METHOD Stir and strain.

GARNISH Twist of lemon.

GLASS Standard cocktail (140 mL).

Gin-and-It
(International)

45 mL	Gin	3	/4
15 mL	Sweet red 'Italian'		
	vermouth	1	/4
	Ice		

METHOD Stir and strain.

GARNISH Cherry.

GLASS Martini (90 mL).

Gin Fizz
(International)

45 mL	Gin	3	/6
30 mL	Lemon juice (fresh)	2	/6
15 mL	Sugar syrup	1	/6
	Soda		
	Ice		

METHOD Shake and strain the gin, lemon juice, and sugar syrup. Add two or three cubes of ice to the glass. Top with soda.

GARNISH Long straws.

GLASS Highball (300 mL).

NOTE Fizzes can be made with brandy or whisky instead of gin. Some fizzes are made using an egg, or different parts of an egg: see Golden Fizz, Royal Fizz, and Silver Fizz.

Gin Sling
(International)

45 mL	Gin	3	/6
30 mL	Lemon juice	2	/6
15 mL	Sugar syrup	1	/6
	Soda		
	Ice		

METHOD Build all ingredients into a Highball glass half-filled with ice. Stir and top with soda.

GARNISH Slice of lemon and a cherry.

GLASS Highball (300 mL).

Gin Squash
(International)

30 mL	Gin	2	/3
15 mL	Lemon cordial	1	/3
	Lemonade or soda		
	Ice		

METHOD Half fill a Highball glass with ice. Add the gin and top with lemonade or soda, leaving room for the lemon cordial. Add lemon cordial. Stir.

GARNISH Slice of lemon and straws.

GLASS Highball (300 mL).

Glühwein or Mulled Wine
(International)

1500 mL	Red wine (two bottles)	12	/23
750 mL	Ruby port (one bottle)	6	/23
375 mL	Brandy	3	/23
250 mL	Water	2	/23
250g	Seedless raisins		
200g	Sugar		
12	Cloves		
6	Cinnamon sticks		
1	Crushed whole nutmeg		
	Peel of 2 oranges		
	Peel of 2 lemons		
	Almonds		

METHOD Put the peel, cloves, cinnamon sticks, sugar, nutmeg and water into a saucepan. (Note that the nutmeg should be crushed, not grated.) Bring to the boil and boil for five minutes. Strain. Add the brandy, red wine, port and raisins. Heat but do not boil. Place one almond into each glass. Pour or ladle mixture into glasses, ensuring that each glass contains some raisins.

GARNISH No garnish.

GLASS Stemmed glass or mug with handles (approx. 150 mL).

SERVES Twenty.

NOTE Glühwein or Mulled Wine is usually served when the weather is cold, for example in the snowfields after skiing.

Godfather
(International)

45 mL	Scotch whisky	9	/13
20 mL	Amaretto di Saronno	4	/13
	Ice		

METHOD Build into an ice-filled glass.

GARNISH Optional.

GLASS Old Fashioned (180-240 mL).

Godmother
(International)

45 mL	Vodka	9	/13
20 mL	Amaretto di Saronno	4	/13
	Ice		

METHOD Build into an ice-filled glass.

GARNISH Optional.

GLASS Old Fashioned (180-240 mL).

Golden Cadillac
(International)

30 mL	Galliano	1	/3
30 mL	White crème de cacao	1	/3
30 mL	Cream	1	/3
	Ice		

METHOD Shake and strain.

GARNISH Strawberry.

GLASS Standard cocktail (140 mL).

Golden Dream, No 1
(International)

30 mL	Galliano	1	/4
30 mL	Cointreau	1	/4
30 mL	Orange juice	1	/4
30 mL	Cream	1	/4
	Ice		

METHOD Shake and strain.

GARNISH Cherry (optional).

GLASS Tulip flute (180 mL).

Golden Dream, No 2
(Australian)

15 mL	Galliano	1	/7
15 mL	Cointreau	1	/7
15 mL	Orange juice	1	/7
60 mL	Cream	4	/7
	Ice		

METHOD Shake and strain.

GARNISH Sugar-frosted strawberry and chocolate flakes.

GLASS Tulip flute (180 mL).

NOTE The main difference between the international and Australian versions of the Golden Dream is that the Australian one has a very much higher proportion of cream.

Golden Fizz
(International)

30 mL	Gin	2	/5
30 mL	Lemon juice	2	/5
15 mL	Sugar syrup	1	/5
1	Egg yolk		
	Soda		
	Ice		

METHOD Shake and strain the gin, lemon juice, sugar syrup and egg yolk. Add two or three cubes of ice to the glass. Top with soda.

GARNISH Long straws.

GLASS Highball (300 mL).

NOTE Care must be taken when adding the soda or the drink may FIZZ over the side! Compare Royal Fizz and Silver Fizz.

Golden Dream

Golden Glory
(Australian)

15 mL	Peach liqueur	1	/8
15 mL	Strawberry liqueur	1	/8
30 mL	Apple juice	2	/8
60 mL	Orange juice	4	/8

Ice

METHOD Shake and strain over ice.

 GARNISH Orange wheel.

GLASS Standard cocktail (140 mL).

From the Country Club Casino, Launceston, Tasmania.

Golden Glow
(Australian)

45 mL	Scotch whisky	3	/6
15 mL	Dark rum	1	/6
15 mL	Orange juice	1	/6
15 mL	Lemon juice	1	/6
5 mL	Grenadine		

Ice

METHOD Shake and strain all ingredients except grenadine into glass. Pour grenadine on top.

GARNISH Cherry.

GLASS Standard cocktail (140 mL).

Golden Guytime
(Australian)

30 mL	Butterscotch schnapps	2	/6
15 mL	Tia Maria	1	/6
15 mL	Bailey's Irish Cream	1	/6
30 mL	Cream	2	/6

Ice

METHOD Shake and strain.

 GARNISH Frost glass with crushed sweet biscuit and crushed nuts.

GLASS Large champagne saucer.

Created by Mark Filgate.

Golden Nipple
(Shooter)
(Australian)

20 mL	Galliano	1	/3
20 mL	Bailey's Irish Cream	1	/3
20 mL	Cream (optional)	1	/3

METHOD Layer in the above order.

GARNISH No garnish.

GLASS Shot (60 mL).

Golden Orchid
(Australian)

30 mL	Scotch whisky	2	/5
30 mL	Bols advocaat	2	/5
15 mL	Bols maraschino	1	/5

Ice

METHOD Shake and strain.

GARNISH Maraschino cherry.

GLASS Standard cocktail (140 mL).

Created by Russell Steabben. Winner of the ABG National Competition, 1966.

Golden Scream
(Mocktail)
(Australian)

30 mL	Sugar syrup	2	/7
15 mL	Orange juice	1	/7
60 mL	Cream	4	/7

Ice

METHOD Shake and strain.

GARNISH Strawberry and chocolate flakes.

GLASS Standard cocktail (140 mL).

Gone Troppo
(Australian)

45 mL	Seagram's peach liqueur	9	/22
35 mL	Seagram's banana liqueur	7	/22
30 mL	Pineapple juice	6	/22

3	Fresh strawberries
1 scoop	Ice

METHOD Blend peach liqueur, banana liqueur, ice and strawberries. Float pineapple juice on top.

GARNISH Pineapple wedge and a cherry, and two pineapple leaves.

GLASS Tulip flute (180 mL).

Created by Roy Hopgood. Winner of the ABG South Australian Competition, 1988.

Grasshopper, No 1
(International)

30 mL	Green crème de menthe	1	/3
30 mL	White crème de cacao	1	/3
30 mL	Cream	1	/3

Ice

METHOD Shake and strain.

GARNISH Maraschino cherry.

GLASS Standard cocktail (140 mL).

Grasshopper, No 2
(Australian)

30 mL	Green crème de menthe	1	/4
30 mL	White crème de cacao	1	/4
60 mL	Cream	2	/4

Ice

METHOD Shake and strain.

GARNISH Maraschino cherry and short straws.

GLASS Standard cocktail (140 mL).

Greek Tycoon
(Shooter)
(Australian)

15 mL	Sambuca	1	/3
15 mL	Ouzo	1	/3
15 mL	Tequila	1	/3

METHOD Layer in the above order.

GARNISH No garnish.

GLASS Shot (60 mL).

Group Sex
(Australian)

60 mL	Frangelico	1	/3
60 mL	Kahlua	1	/3
60 mL	Malibu	1	/3

5-10 mL	Grenadine
	Milk
	Cream
	Ice

METHOD Build liqueurs over ice. Dribble the grenadine down the inside of the glass. Top with a mixture of equal quantities of cream and milk.

GARNISH No garnish.

GLASS Colada (400 mL).

From Sheraton Towers, Southgate, Melbourne.

Hair-of-the-Dog
(Pick-me-up)
(International)

60 mL	Scotch whisky	2	/5
60 mL	Cream	2	/5
30 mL	Honey	1	/5

Ice

METHOD Shake and strain. Fill glass with ice. Pour ingredients in.

GARNISH No garnish.

GLASS Old Fashioned (180-240 mL).

Hard On

(Shooter)
(Australian)

15 mL	Kahlua	1	/3
15 mL	Lena banana liqueur	1	/3
15 mL	Bailey's Irish Cream	1	/3

METHOD Layer in the above order.

GARNISH No garnish.

GLASS Shot (60 mL).

Harlequin

(Australian)

30 mL	Cognac	2	/3
15 mL	Grand Marnier	1	/3
	Ice		

METHOD Stir and strain.

GARNISH Frost glass with alternate strips of instant coffee and sugar, i.e. two quarters of the rim frosted with instant coffee and two quarters with sugar. Arrange the coffee and sugar in a dish in quarters before placing the glass in it to frost it. (See Section 4, Garnish 15.) Cherry.

GLASS Standard cocktail (140 mL) or Martini (90 mL).

Created by Sir Ian Orton.

Harvey Cowpuncher

(Australian)

30 mL	Vodka	2	/3
15 mL	Galliano	1	/3
	Milk		
	Ice		

METHOD Build vodka and milk over ice. Float the Galliano on top.

GARNISH Orange wheel and a cherry.

GLASS Highball (300 mL).

Harvey Wallbanger, No 1

(International)

30 mL	Vodka	1	/3
60 mL	Orange juice	2	/3
2 tsps	Galliano		
	Ice		

METHOD Build vodka and orange juice over ice. Float two teaspoons of Galliano on top.

GARNISH Long straws, orange wheel and a cherry.

GLASS Old Fashioned (180-240 mL).

Harvey Wallbanger, No 2

(Australian)

30 mL	Vodka	2	/3
15 mL	Galliano	1	/3
	Orange juice		
	Ice		

METHOD Fill a Highball glass three-quarters full with cubed ice. Pour in vodka. Top with orange juice. Stir. Float Galliano on top.

GARNISH Long straws, half slice of orange and a cherry.

GLASS Highball (300 mL).

NOTE A Harvey Wallbanger is now usually served with straws, but traditionally the vodka and orange mix was drunk without straws through the floating Galliano.

Highball

See Whiskey Highball.

Harlequin

Holiday Egg-nog
(Punch)
(International)

1 litre	Cream (cold)	20 /50
750 mL	Bourbon whiskey	15 /50
400 mL	Milk (cold)	8 /50
350 mL	Jamaica rum	7 /50

10	Egg whites
10	Egg yolks
6 tblsp	Castor sugar
1	Grated orange rind
1	Grated lemon rind
1	Ground nutmeg
	Punch-bowl (3-litre)

METHOD Place the egg whites in a large mixing bowl and add three (only) tablespoons of sugar. Beat the egg whites and castor sugar with a wire whisk or an electric rotary beater until they thicken. In another large bowl, beat the egg yolks until they thicken. Pour the foamy egg whites and sugar into the beaten egg yolks and beat them together until they are thoroughly combined.

Place the cream (which should be cold) and three more tablespoons of castor sugar in a three-litre punch-bowl and beat until the cream doubles in volume. Now, beating constantly, slowly pour the egg mixture into the punch-bowl with the whipped cream. When the whipped cream and the egg mixture have thoroughly combined, slowly add the bourbon and the rum and then the cold milk, beating all the while. By this time the egg-nog will have thickened a little; it will thicken even more as it chills. Sprinkle the top with grated lemon and orange peel and the ground nutmeg and chill for at least two hours, preferably overnight.

 GLASS Wine glass (240 mL) or Highball (300 mL).

SERVES Fifteen.

Holly Berry
(Australian)

30 mL	Brandy	2 /5
30 mL	Midori melon liqueur	2 /5
15 mL	Dry vermouth	1 /5
	Cream	
	Ice	

METHOD Shake and strain cognac, Midori melon liqueur, and dry vermouth. Float cream on top.

 GARNISH Cherry.

GLASS Standard cocktail (140 mL).

Honey Bear, No 1
(Australian)

15 mL	Frangelico	1 /5
15 mL	Kahlua	1 /5
15 mL	Milk	1 /5
15 mL	Cream	1 /5
15 mL	Honey	1 /5
	Ice	

METHOD Blend.

 GARNISH Cherry.

GLASS Balloon.

Honey Bear, No 2
(Shooter)
(Australian)

15 mL	Frangelico	1 /4
15 mL	Tia Maria	1 /4
15 mL	Cream	1 /4
15 mL	Honey	1 /4

METHOD Layer in the above order.

GARNISH No garnish.

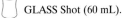 GLASS Shot (60 mL).

Harvey Wallbanger

Honeyed Nuts
(Australian)

30 mL	Frangelico	2	/6
15 mL	Kahlua	1	/6
15 mL	Advocaat	1	/6
30 mL	Honey	2	/6

120 mL Cream
Ice

METHOD Blend.

GARNISH Frost glass with crushed hazelnuts and honey.

GLASS Balloon (285 mL).

Created by Alan Newbold, 1993.

Hopscotch
(Australian)

30 mL	Butterscotch schnapps	1	/5
30 mL	Brown crème de cacao	1	/5
60 mL	Cream	2	/5
30 mL	Milk	1	/5

Half tsp Malt
Ice

METHOD Blend.

GARNISH Strawberry and shaved chocolate.

GLASS Tulip flute (180 mL).

From the Park Royal, Brisbane.

Horse's Neck
(International)

30 mL Brandy
4 drops Angostura bitters (optional)
Dry ginger ale
Ice

METHOD Hang lemon spiral in glass. Add ice to fill glass. Build brandy and bitters over ice. Top with dry ginger ale.

GARNISH Whole spiral lemon peel hung by neck into glass, long straw.

GLASS Highball (300 mL).

Iced Apple Tea
(Mocktail)
(Australian)

Cold tea
30 mL Lemon juice
Apple juice
Ice

METHOD Build lemon juice over ice. Top with equal amounts of pre-prepared cold tea and apple juice.

GARNISH No garnish.

GLASS Highball (300 mL).

Iced Coffee
(Mocktail)
(International)

90-120 mL	Pre-made cold coffee
90 mL	Milk
30 mL	Cream
2 scoops	Ice-cream
	Cream (whipped)
1/4 scoop	Ice

METHOD Blend coffee, milk, pouring cream and one scoop of ice-cream. Pour into glass and add one scoop of ice-cream. Float whipped cream on top.

GARNISH Chocolate flakes.

GLASS Coffee glass or mug.

Iced Tea
(Mocktail)
(International)

5 mL Lemon juice
Pre-made cold tea
Ice

METHOD Build.

GARNISH Lemon wheel and sugar cube.

GLASS Highball (300 mL).

Illusion
See Midori Illusion.

Horse's Neck

I'm Driving
(Mocktail)
(Australian)

120 mL	Orange juice	2	/3
60 mL	Cream	1	/3
1	Small banana		
1 scoop	Ice		

METHOD Blend.

GARNISH Orange wheel and a cherry.

GLASS Balloon (285 mL).

Irish Coffee
(International)

30 mL	Irish whiskey
	Sugar (to taste)
	Coffee (piping hot)
	Cream (lightly whipped)

METHOD Mix sugar and Irish whiskey in a stemmed glass or mug with a handle. Pour the piping hot coffee over the back of a barspoon. This will ensure that the glass will not crack. Carefully pour the cream over the back of a spoon.

GARNISH Coffee bean.

GLASS Irish Coffee (with stem or handle).

NOTE When taking the order, ask your customers how much sugar they usually take in their coffee. See also Liqueur Coffees and Roman Coffee.

Italian Stallion
(Australian)

30 mL	Banana liqueur	1	/4
30 mL	Galliano	1	/4
60 mL	Cream	2	/4
	Ice		

METHOD Shake and strain.

GARNISH Grated chocolate.

GLASS Standard cocktail (140 mL)

Jaffa
(Australian)

30 mL	Kahlua	2	/7
15 mL	Scotch whisky	1	/7
15 mL	Grand Marnier	1	/7
15 mL	Orange juice	1	/7
30 mL	Cream	2	/7
	Ice		

METHOD Shake and strain.

GARNISH Chocolate frost.

GLASS Standard cocktail (140 mL).

Japanese Slipper
(Australian)

30 mL	Midori melon liqueur	1	/3
30 mL	Cointreau	1	/3
30 mL	Lemon juice	1	/3
	Ice		

METHOD Shake and strain.

GARNISH Cherry (optional).

GLASS Standard cocktail (140 mL).

NOTE A Japanese Slipper can be served on-the-rocks.

Created by Jean-Paul Bourguignon in Melbourne in 1984. It has become one of the most popular cocktails in Australia.

Jellybean
(Australian)

30 mL	Ouzo	3	/4
10 mL	Raspberry cordial	1	/4
	Lemonade		
	Ice		

METHOD Place ice in glass, add ouzo, and top with lemonade. Pour in raspberry cordial.

GARNISH Long straws.

GLASS Highball (300 mL).

NOTE You can make a Black Jellybean by substituting cola for lemonade.

Japanese Slipper

Jerry Lewis Special
(Australian)

30 mL	Stolichnaya vodka	1	/2
30 mL	Midori melon liqueur	1	/2
5 mL	Blue curaçao		
	Ice		

METHOD Stir vodka and Midori over ice and strain into glass. Gently pour curaçao through.

GARNISH No garnish.

GLASS Martini (90 mL).

From the Dean Martin Club, Sydney.

John Collins
See Tom Collins.

Junger Stern
(Australian)

30 mL	Midori melon liqueur	2	/3
15 mL	Lena Banana liqueur	1	/3
3	Pureed strawberries		
4	Pineapple pieces		
Half a	Passionfruit (pulp)		
1 scoop	Ice		

METHOD Pour strawberry purée the full length of the Highball glass, keeping the glass almost horizontal. Blend all other ingredients and pour into the glass carefully so as to leave the purée as a stripe down the side of the glass.

GARNISH Slice of star fruit (carambola), cherry and pineapple leaves.

GLASS Highball (300 mL).

Created by Ingram Jung, 1993.

Kakuri
(Australian)

15 mL	Suntory mango liqueur	1	/4
30 mL	Pimm's No 1 cup	2	/4
15 mL	Bianco vermouth	1	/4
5 mL	Lemon juice		
	Ice		

METHOD Stir and strain.

GARNISH Lemon peel rose and a sprig of mint.

GLASS Martini (90 mL).

NOTE *Kakuri* is an Aboriginal word meaning 'dry'.

Created by Raymond Hopgood, 1993.

Kamikaze
(International)

30 mL	Vodka	1	/3
30 mL	Cointreau	1	/3
30 mL	Lemon juice	1	/3
5 mL	Lime cordial		
	Ice		

METHOD Shake and strain.

GARNISH Red cocktail onion.

GLASS Standard cocktail (140 mL).

K.G.B.
(International)

30 mL	Kahlua	1	/3
30 mL	Grand Marnier	1	/3
30 mL	Bailey's Irish Cream	1	/3
	Ice		

METHOD Build.

GARNISH No garnish.

GLASS Old Fashioned (180-240 mL).

King Alfonso
(International)

30 mL   Kahlua
        Cream (whipped)
        Ice

METHOD Fill glass with ice. Build
Kahlua over. Top with whipped cream.
Do not stir.

GARNISH No garnish.

GLASS Old Fashioned (180-240 mL).

Kir
(International)

15 mL   Crème de cassis
        Dry white wine (chilled)

METHOD Build measure of crème de
cassis into empty glass (no ice). Top with
white wine.

GARNISH No garnish.

GLASS Flute (180 mL).

Kir Imperial
(International)

15 mL   Crème de framboise
        Sparkling wine (méthode
        champenoise) (chilled)

METHOD Build measure of crème de
framboise into empty glass (no ice). Top
with sparkling wine.

GARNISH No garnish.

GLASS Flute (180 mL).

Kir Royale
(International)

15 mL   Crème de cassis
        Sparkling wine
        (méthode champenoise)(chilled)

METHOD Build measure of crème de
cassis into empty glass (no ice). Top with
sparkling wine.

GARNISH No garnish.

GLASS Flute (180 mL).

Kiss my Asteroid
(Australian)

30 mL	Midori melon liqueur	2	/5
15 mL	Cointreau	1	/5
30 mL	Blue curaçao	2	/5

        Cubed ice
        Pineapple juice
        Crushed ice

METHOD Build Midori, Cointreau and
pineapple juice over cubed ice. Add the
blue curaçao to one large scoop of
crushed ice and float it on top of the
pineapple juice.

GARNISH No garnish.

GLASS Colada (400 mL).

Kool Cat
(Australian)

30 mL	Kahlua	2	/4
15 mL	Green crème de menthe	1	/4
15 mL	White crème de cacao	1	/4

        Milk
        Ice

METHOD Build. Top with milk.

GARNISH Two cherries.

GLASS Highball (300 mL).

Lamborghini

See Flaming Lamborghini

Lamington

(Shooter)
(Australian)

20 mL	Malibu	1	/2
20 mL	Brown crème de cacao	1	/2

2 drops Advocaat

METHOD Layer Malibu and crème de cacao. Add drops of advocaat.

GARNISH No garnish.

GLASS Shot (60 mL).

Lazy Lizard

(Australian)

30 mL	Brown crème de cacao	2	/8
15 mL	Bailey's Irish Cream	1	/8
15 mL	Frangelico	1	/8
60 mL	Cream	4	/8

Ice

METHOD Shake and strain.

GARNISH Half strawberry, chocolate dust.

GLASS Standard cocktail (140 mL).

From the Colonial Club Resort, Poolside, Cairns, Queensland.

Lemonade

(Mocktail)
(International)

30 mL	Lemon juice, (freshly squeezed)	1	/5
120 mL	Sugar syrup	4	/5

Ice

METHOD Build.

GARNISH Wheels of lemon.

GLASS Highball (300mL).

Lemon and Lime Shake

(Mocktail)
(International)

60 mL	Lime cordial	4	/5
15 mL	Lemon juice	1	/5

Half	Egg white

Ice

METHOD Shake and strain.

GARNISH Cherry.

GLASS Standard cocktail (140 mL).

Lemon, Lime and Bitters

(Mocktail)
(Australian)

4 drops Angostura bitters
Lemonade
10 mL Lime cordial

Ice

METHOD Roll the bitters around the inside of the glass. Expel any excess. Place the ice in the glass. Add the lemonade. Leave enough room for the lime cordial to be added last. The weight of the cordial will ensure that it mixes through the drink.

GARNISH Lemon wheel.

GLASS Highball (300 mL).

Lip Sip Suck
(International)

30 mL   Tequila
        Salt
        Lemon

METHOD
Step 1 Lick the salt.

Step 2 Skull the tequila.

Step 3 Suck the lemon.

 GARNISH No garnish.

GLASS Shot (60 mL).

NOTE This is not strictly a cocktail, but is the traditional (slammer) method of drinking tequila.

Liqueur Coffees
(International)

Today bartenders serve an extensive range of liqueur coffees as alternatives to the traditional Irish Coffee. They are given all sorts of names; often they are named after the establishment where they are being served. Liqueurs commonly served in coffee include:

    Bénédictine
    Cointreau
    Galliano
    Kahlua
    Tia Maria

 METHOD See Irish Coffee.

GLASS Irish coffee with stem or handle.

NOTE Liqueurs have a much higher sugar content than whiskey, and it is not usually necessary to add sugar to a liqueur coffee.

Liquid Lamington
(Australian)

30 mL	Kahlua	2	/7
30 mL	Malibu	2	/7
15 mL	Bailey's Irish Cream	1	/7
30 mL	Cream	2	/7

Ice

METHOD Blend.

GARNISH Desiccated coconut.

GLASS Standard cocktail (140 mL).

From the Elephant Bar, Royal Hotel, Paddington (Sydney).

Long Island Tea
See New Iced Tea.

Long Sloe Comfortable Screw up against the Wall
(Australian)

30 mL	Vodka	2	/5
15 mL	Southern Comfort	1	/5
15 mL	Sloe gin	1	/5
15 mL	Galliano	1	/5

Orange juice
Ice

METHOD Build spirits and liqueurs over ice. Top with orange juice.

GARNISH Orange wheel with cherry.

GLASS Highball (300 mL).

See also Comfortable Screw and Sloe Comfortable Screw.

Loose Goose, The
(Australian)

Two cocktail shakers are required.

In the first shaker:

30 mL	Midori melon liqueur	1	/5
30 mL	Triple sec	1	/5
90 mL	Pineapple juice	3	/5

Ice

In the second shaker:

60 mL	Cream	4	/5
15 mL	Midori melon liqueur	1/	5

Ice

METHOD Shake and strain both. Pour first shaker into glass until three-quarters full. Float cream mixture from second shaker on top.

 GARNISH Pineapple wedge.

GLASS Colada (400 mL).

From The Loose Goose Bar/Café, Novotel, Brisbane.

Mai Tai, No 1
(International)

20 mL	White rum	2	/10
20 mL	Dark rum	2	/10
20 mL	Cointreau	2	/10
10 mL	Orgeat syrup	1	/10
10 mL	Grenadine	1	/10
20 mL	Lime juice	2	/10

Crushed ice

METHOD Fill glass with crushed ice. Build all ingredients into glass.

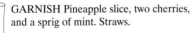 GARNISH Pineapple slice, two cherries, and a sprig of mint. Straws.

GLASS Large Highball (400 mL).

Mai Tai, No 2
(Australian)

15 mL	White rum	3	/25
15 mL	Golden rum	3	/25
15 mL	Tequila	3	/25
15 mL	Triple sec	3	/25
15 mL	Apricot brandy	3	/25
15 mL	Lemon juice (fresh)	3	/25
15 mL	Orange juice (processed)	3	/25
15 mL	Pineapple juice (unsweetened)	3	/25
5 mL	Grenadine	1	/25

1 scoop Ice

METHOD Blend all the ingredients except the grenadine. Pour the mixture into the glass and then add the grenadine.

 GARNISH Pineapple slice, two cherries, and a sprig of mint. Straws.

GLASS Large balloon.

Malfunction
(Australian)

30 mL	Bailey's Irish Cream	2	/5
15 mL	Cointreau	1	/5
15 mL	Grand Marnier	1	/5
15 mL	Galliano	1	/5

Ice

METHOD Fill glass with crushed ice. Build all ingredients into glass.

GARNISH Cherry.

GLASS Standard cocktail (140 mL).

From Waves Sports Bar, Wrest Point Casino, Hobart.

Mango Colada
(Australian)

30 mL	White rum	1	/7
30 mL	Coconut cream	1	/7
30 mL	Mango liqueur	1	/7
90 mL	Pineapple juice	3	/7
30 mL	Cream	1	/7

2 slices Mango
1 scoop Ice

METHOD Place all ingredients into a
blender and blend for about ten seconds.

GARNISH Wedge of pineapple and a
cherry.

GLASS Colada (400 mL).

Mango Daiquiri

See Strawberry Daiquiri, No 2 (note).

Man-Goes-to-Water
(Australian)

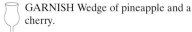

30 mL	Suntory mango liqueur	2	/6
30 mL	Lena banana liqueur	2	/6
15 mL	Bacardi white rum	1	/6
15 mL	Lime juice	1	/6

4 pieces Watermelon (small)
Ice

METHOD Blend.

GARNISH Star fruit and watermelon
slice.

GLASS Colada (400 ml).

Created by Nigel Frawley.

Mango Fizz
(Australian)

30 mL	Mango liqueur	2	/5
30 mL	Lemon juice	2	/5
15 mL	Sugar syrup	1	/5

1   Egg white
1-2 slices Mango
           Soda
           Ice

METHOD Blend all ingredients except
soda. Top with soda.

GARNISH Half strawberry.

GLASS Highball (300 mL).

Mango Madness
(Australian)

30 mL	Mango liqueur	1	/5
30 mL	Advocaat	1	/5
30 mL	Cream	1	/5
60 mL	Orange juice	2	/5

5 mL   Grenadine
Half   Fresh banana
        Ice

METHOD Blend.

GARNISH Banana and a cherry.

GLASS Balloon (285 ml).

From Dominiques Panthers Club, Sydney.

Manhattan
(International)

45 mL	Rye whiskey	9	/13
20 mL	Sweet vermouth	4	/13

2 drops Angostura bitters
        Ice

METHOD Stir and strain.

GARNISH Maraschino cherry.

GLASS Martini (90 mL).

Manhattan, Dry
(International)

Same recipe as for the standard Manhattan (above), except that dry vermouth is used instead of sweet.

METHOD Stir and strain.

 GARNISH Twist of lemon.

GLASS Martini (90 mL).

Mardi Gras
(Australian)

30 mL	Bertram's Van der Hum	2	/5
15 mL	Galliano	1	/5
30 mL	Pineapple juice (unsweetened)	2	/5
1	Egg yolk		
	Ice		

METHOD Shake and strain.

 GARNISH Light sprinkle of cinnamon.

GLASS Standard cocktail (140 mL).

Created by Russell Steabben at the Broadbeach Hotel, Queensland. Winner of the ABG National Competition, 1967.

Margarita, No 1
(International)

30 mL	Tequila	6	/10
15 mL	Cointreau	3	/10
5 mL	Lemon or lime juice	1	/10
	Ice		

METHOD Shake and strain.

 GARNISH Salt-frosted glass.

GLASS Martini (90 mL).

Margarita, No 2
(Australian)

30 mL	Tequila	2	/5
15 mL	Cointreau	1	/5
30 mL	Lemon juice	2	/5
5 mL	Egg white (optional)		
	Ice		

METHOD Shake and strain.

 GARNISH Whole thin slice of lemon, glass frosted with salt.

GLASS Standard cocktail (140 mL).

NOTE In some bars a blender is used. Note also that Margaritas are sometimes served in deep champagne saucers instead of standard cocktail glasses.

Margarita, Frozen
(Australian)

30 mL	Tequila	1	/3
30 mL	Cointreau	1	/3
30 mL	Lemon juice	1	/3
	Ice		

METHOD Blend.

 GARNISH Salt-frosted glass.

GLASS Champagne saucer.

NOTE The Frozen Margarita is mixed in a blender. If the proportions of ice and ingredients are mixed correctly the finished product will resemble shaved ice. For the best results all ingredients, including the glass, should be refrigerated, or kept in the freezer. In order to obtain the desired frozen appearance and consistency, equal proportions of ice and other ingredients should be used. The blender should be on slow speed for about ten seconds.

Manhattan

Martinis

At the turn of the twentieth century the recipe for a Martini was well-established: two parts gin to one part dry vermouth. Over the years since then the drink has tended to become drier, made with more gin and less vermouth. In America the vermouth often almost, or even completely, disappears. In Australia a mix of six parts of gin to one of dry vermouth is now usual. There is also a Sweet Martini variation, which uses sweet vermouth in place of dry. Extra care must be taken when preparing Martinis as regular Martini drinkers are usually very particular about how they like their Martinis made. If in doubt ask the customer. Chilling all ingredients, including the mixing glass, will produce a superior Martini.

Martini, Dry, No 1
(International)

40 mL	Gin (London dry)	4	/5
10 mL	Dry vermouth	1	/5

Ice

METHOD Stir and strain. Place ice in a mixing glass, filling it at least two-thirds full. Pour in the ingredients. Stir gently for about five seconds until all the ingredients are cold. Strain into a chilled glass.

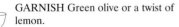 GARNISH Green olive or a twist of lemon.

GLASS Martini (90 mL).

NOTE Martinis can be served on-the-rocks.

Martini, Dry, No 2
(Australian)

30 mL	Gin (London dry)	6	/7
5 mL	Dry vermouth	1	/7

Ice

METHOD Same as for international recipe.

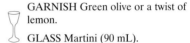 GARNISH Green olive or a twist of lemon.

GLASS Martini (90 mL).

Martini Mocktail
(Australian)

15 mL	Lime cordial	1	/5
60 mL	Tonic water	4	/5

Ice

METHOD Stir and strain.

GARNISH Green olive.

GLASS Standard cocktail (140 mL).

Martini, Perfect
(International)

60 mL	Gin	6	/8
10 mL	Sweet red vermouth	1	/8
10 mL	Dry vermouth	1	/8

Ice

METHOD Stir and strain.

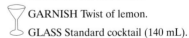 GARNISH Twist of lemon.

GLASS Standard cocktail (140 mL).

Margarita

Martini, Sweet
(International)

40 mL	Gin	4	/5
10 mL	Sweet red vermouth	1	/5
	Ice		

METHOD Stir and strain. Place ice in a mixing glass, filling it at least two-thirds full. Pour in the ingredients. Stir gently for about five seconds until all the ingredients are cold. Strain into a chilled glass.

 GARNISH Cherry or an olive.

GLASS Martini (90 mL).

Martini Variation
(Australian)

30 mL	Gin	6	/9
5 mL	Dry vermouth	1	/9
10 mL	Selected liqueur or spirit	2	/9

METHOD Stir and strain.

 GARNISH Cherry or olive depending upon variation selected.

GLASS Martini (90 mL).

NOTE The most common and popular variation is to use Campari. Liqueurs are also popular, Midori and mango liqueur for example.

See also Gibson, Tequini and Vodkatini.

Melon Ball
(Australian)

45 mL	Midori melon liqueur	3	/5
30 mL	Vodka	2	/5
	Pineapple juice		
	Ice		

METHOD Build. Top with pineapple juice.

GARNISH Pineapple wedge.

GLASS Highball (300 mL).

Melon Bullet, No 1
(Shooter)
(Australian)

| 20 mL | Midori melon liqueur | 1 | /2 |
| 20 mL | Triple sec | 1 | /2 |

2 drops Blue curaçao

METHOD Layer Midori and triple sec. Add drops of curaçao.

GARNISH No garnish.

GLASS Shot (60 mL).

Melon Bullet, No 2
(Shooter)
(Australian)

15 mL	Midori melon liqueur	1	/4
15 mL	White rum	1	/4
15 mL	Lemon juice	1	/4
15 mL	Cointreau	1	/4

METHOD Layer in the above order.

GARNISH No garnish.

GLASS Shot (60 mL).

Melon Fizz
(Australian)

15 mL	Midori melon liqueur	1	/4
30 mL	Lemon juice	2	/4
15 mL	Sugar syrup	1	/4
1	Egg white		
1 slice	Honeydew melon		
	Soda		
	Ice		

METHOD Blend all ingredients except soda. Top with soda.

GARNISH Half strawberry.

GLASS Highball (300 mL).

Martini

Ménage à Trois

(Champagne cocktail)
(Australian)

15 mL	Monin Triple Lime liqueur	1	/2
15 mL	Cointreau	1	/2

Sparkling wine
(méthode champenoise)

METHOD Chill the liqueurs in a mixing glass. Strain into the glass. Top with sparkling wine.

 GARNISH Orangé spiral.

GLASS Flute (180 ml).

Created by Frank Corsar. Winner of Liquid Art National Cocktail Competition, 1986.

Mickey Mouse

(Mocktail)
(International)

Cola
2 tblsp Ice-cream
1 tblsp Cream (whipped)

METHOD Place one tablespoon of ice-cream in the glass. Add 10 mL of cola. Blend carefully with a bar spoon. Top with cola. Be very careful that the drink does not foam over the rim. Add the second tablespoon of ice-cream and top with whipped cream.

GARNISH Shaved chocolate, long straws.

GLASS Highball (300 mL).

NOTE Serve on a plate with a doily.

Midnight Rose

(Australian)

30 mL	Seagram's advocaat	2	/6
15 mL	Seagram's strawberry liqueur	1	/6
15 mL	Seagram's kirsch	1	/6
30 mL	Cream	2	/6

METHOD Shake and strain.

GARNISH Half strawberry.

GLASS Standard cocktail (140 mL).

Created by Julius Pek, 1988.

Midori Alexander

(Australian)

30 mL	Midori melon liqueur	1	/4
30 mL	White crème de cacao	1	/4
60 mL	Cream	2	/4

Ice

METHOD Shake and strain.

GARNISH Sprinkle of nutmeg.

GLASS Standard cocktail (140 mL).

Midori-and-Cointreau Frappé

(Australian)

15 mL	Midori melon liqueur	1	/2
15 mL	Cointreau	1	/2

Crushed ice

METHOD Fill glass with crushed ice. Build Midori and Cointreau over. (See Frappés.)

 GARNISH Cherry, two short straws.

GLASS Standard cocktail (140 mL).

Midori Colada
(Australian)

30 mL	Midori melon liqueur	1	/7
30 mL	White rum	1	/7
30 mL	Coconut cream	1	/7
30 mL	Cream	1	/7
90 mL	Pineapple juice	3	/7

1 slice Pineapple (or honeydew melon)
1 scoop Ice

METHOD Blend.

GARNISH Pineapple wedge and cherry.

GLASS Colada (400 mL).

Midori Illusion, No 1
(Australian)

30 mL	Midori melon liqueur	2	/9
30 mL	Cointreau	2	/9
30 mL	Vodka	2	/9
45 mL	Lemon juice	3	/9

Ice

METHOD Shake and strain.

GARNISH No garnish.

GLASS Standard cocktail (140 mL).

Midori Illusion, No 2
(Australian)

60 mL	Midori	4	/12
15 mL	Vodka	1	/12
15 mL	Cointreau	1	/12
60 mL	Pineapple juice	4	/12
30 mL	Lemon Juice	2	/12

Ice

METHOD Shake and strain.

GARNISH No garnish.

GLASS Shot (60 ml).

NOTE This drink is served in the shaker and empty shot glasses are supplied. The customers pour the cocktail into the glasses themselves.

Midori Melon Punch
(Australian)

500 mL	Midori melon liqueur	10	/35
150 mL	Lena banana liqueur	3	/35
500 mL	Vodka	10	/35
600 mL	Cream	12	/35

1 punnet   Strawberries
2 bottles
Sparkling wine
10 scoops   Ice

METHOD Mix all ingredients except the sparkling wine, the strawberries and the ice in a punchbowl. Add the ice and top with sparkling wine. Clean the strawberries and slice them in half. Garnish the bowl with them.

GLASS Large wine (240 mL).

SERVES Twenty.

Midori Splice
(Australian)

45 mL	Midori melon liqueur	3	/14
30 mL	Malibu	2	/14
120 mL	Pineapple juice	8	/14
15 mL	Cream	1	/14

Ice

METHOD Build Midori, Malibu and pineapple juice. Float cream on top.

GARNISH Pineapple wedge and a cherry.

GLASS Balloon (285 mL).

Mimosa

See Buck's Fizz.

Mint Julep
(International)

60 mL	Bourbon whiskey
1 barsp	Castor sugar
30 mL	Water
4-5 leaves	Fresh mint
	Crushed ice
	Soda (optional)

METHOD Muddle the mint, sugar and water in the glass until the sugar is dissolved. Add the bourbon and fill the glass to the top with crushed ice.

GARNISH Mint leaves.

GLASS Highball (300 mL).

Mission Impossible
(Shooter)
(Australian)

15 mL	Kahlua	1	/4
15 mL	Bailey's Irish Cream	1	/4
15 mL	Cream	1	/4
15 mL	Green Chartreuse	1	/4

METHOD Layer in the above order.

GARNISH No garnish.

GLASS Shot (60 mL).

Mocktails
See individual mocktails (listed under 'mocktails' in index).

Monk's Madness
(Australian)

20 mL	Seagram's strawberry liqueur	4	/25
30 mL	Seagram's brown crème de cacao	6	/25
15 mL	Bénédictine	3	/25
60 mL	Cream	12	/25
	Ice		

METHOD Shake and strain.

GARNISH Chocolate flake frost and a cherry.

GLASS Standard cocktail (140 mL).

Created by Kate Canaway, 1988.

Moscow Mule
(International)

30 mL	Vodka	2	/3
15 mL	Lime cordial	1	/3
	Ginger beer		
	Ice		

METHOD Build vodka and lime cordial into an ice-filled Highball glass. Top with ginger beer.

GARNISH Slice of lime and sprig of mint. Straws.

GLASS Highball (300 mL).

Multiple Orgasm
(Australian)

30 mL	Bailey's Irish Cream	1	/3
30 mL	Cointreau	1	/3
30 mL	Cream	1	/3
	Ice		

METHOD Build.

GARNISH Cherries and a strawberry.

GLASS Balloon (285 mL).

Midori Splice

M.X. Missile
(Shooter)
(Australian)

15 mL	Kahlua	1	/3
15 mL	Bailey's Irish Cream	1	/3
15 mL	Malibu	1	/3

METHOD Layer in the above order.

GARNISH No garnish.

GLASS Shot (60 mL).

Negroni
(International)

30 mL	Gin	1	/3
30 mL	Sweet red vermouth	1	/3
30 mL	Campari	1	/3

Soda (optional)
Ice

METHOD Build over ice. Add soda if desired.

GARNISH Half slice of orange.

GLASS Old Fashioned (240 mL).

New Iced Tea
(Australian)

30 mL	Vodka	1	/5
30 mL	Cointreau	1	/5
30 mL	Tequila	1	/5
30 mL	White rum	1	/5
30 mL	Grapefruit or lemon juice	1	/5

Cola (to colour)
Ice

METHOD Fill the glass with ice and pour all the other ingredients over the ice. Use the cola to colour the drink so that it looks like tea.

GARNISH Sprig of mint.

GLASS Highball (300 mL).

NOTE Also called Long Island Tea.

No Hangover Punch
(Mocktail)
(Australian)

30 mL	Lemon juice	2	/8
15 mL	Grenadine	1	/8
15 mL	Cherry juice	1	/8
15 mL	Sugar syrup	1	/8
30 mL	Pineapple juice	2	/8
15 mL	Orange juice	1	/8

4 drops Angostura bitters
Soda
Ice

METHOD Build. Top with soda.

GARNISH Orange wheel with cherry. Pineapple leaf.

GLASS Colada (400 mL).

Non-Alcoholic Cocktails
See Mocktails (listed under 'mocktails' in index).

Nuts about You
(Australian)

30 mL	Frangelico	2	/12
15 mL	Kahlua	1	/12
15 mL	Advocaat	1	/12
30 mL	Honey	2	/12
90 mL	Cream	6	/12

Ice

METHOD Blend.

GARNISH Strawberry.

GLASS Old Fashioned (240 mL).

From the Holiday Inn, Cairns, Queensland.

Nutty Irishman
(Australian)

30 mL	Frangelico	1	/4
30 mL	Bailey's Irish Cream	1	/4
60 mL	Cream	2	/4

Ice

METHOD Shake and strain.

GARNISH Chocolate sprinkle.

GLASS Standard cocktail (140 mL).

Old Fashioned, No 1
(International)

30 mL	Rye whiskey	6	/8
5 mL	Angostura bitters	1	/8
5 mL	Soda	1	/8

1 cube Sugar
          Ice cubes

METHOD Place sugar in glass. Add Angostura bitters and a dash of soda. Muddle. Fill glass with ice. Add whiskey. Stir.

GARNISH Half slice of orange and two cherries.

GLASS Old Fashioned (180-240 mL).

Old Fashioned, No 2
(Australian)

60 mL	Rye whiskey	1	/2
60 mL	Soda	1	/2

1 cube Sugar
          Angostura bitters
          Ice cubes

METHOD Place the sugar cube on a cutting board and sprinkle a few drops of Angostura bitters onto it. Put the sugar cube into the glass. Add a few cubes of ice. Then add the rye whiskey and top with soda. Stir.

GARNISH Half slice of orange and a cherry.

GLASS Old Fashioned (180-240 mL).

Olé
(Australian)

45 mL	Tequila	9	/16
30 mL	Lena banana liqueur	6	/16
5 mL	Bols blue curaçao	1	/16

Ice

METHOD Stir and strain the tequila and the Lena banana liqueur. Pour into the glass and then add the blue curaçao.

GARNISH One whole lime slice on rim of glass with half of a melon ball on either side secured together with a toothpick

GLASS Standard cocktail (140 mL).

Created by Frank McDermott. Winner of the ABG National Competition (Pre-dinner Cocktail), 1987, and the IBA World Championship, Rome, 1987.

Orange Cadillac
(Australian)

30 mL	Galliano	2	/6
15 mL	White crème de cacao	1	/6
15 mL	Orange juice	1	/6
30 mL	Cream	2	/6

Ice

METHOD Blend.

GARNISH Two straws.

GLASS Flute (180 ml).

Orgasm
(Australian)

30 mL	Cointreau	1	/2
30 mL	Bailey's Irish Cream	1	/2

Ice

METHOD Pour the ingredients into the glass over ice (on-the-rocks).

GARNISH One strawberry and two cherries in the glass.

GLASS Balloon (285 mL).

Paintbox

(Shooter)
(Australian)

15 mL	Cherry advocaat	1	/3
15 mL	Blue curaçao	1	/3
15 mL	Advocaat	1	/3

METHOD Layer in the above order.

GARNISH No garnish.

GLASS Shot (60 mL).

Pan Galactic Gargle Blaster

(Australian)

10 mL	Vodka	1	/9
10 mL	Bacardi white rum	1	/9
10 mL	Gin	1	/9
10 mL	Tequila	1	/9
10 mL	Jack Daniel's whiskey	1	/9
10 mL	Kahlua	1	/9
10 mL	Cointreau	1	/9
10 mL	Galliano	1	/9
10 mL	Cream	1	/9
	Grenadine		
	Ice		

METHOD Shake and strain.

GARNISH Make a grenadine cross on top of the drink.

GLASS Standard cocktail (140 mL).

From Sheraton Towers Southgate, Melbourne.

Paradise

(International)

30 mL	Gin	6	/10
15 mL	Apricot brandy	3	/10
5 mL	Orange juice	1	/10
	Ice		

METHOD Shake and strain.

GARNISH Half slice of orange and a cherry.

GLASS Martini (90 mL).

Parson's Special

(Mocktail)
(International)

60 mL	Orange juice	6	/7
10 mL	Grenadine	1	/7
	Soda		
1	Egg yolk		
	Ice		

METHOD Shake and strain into ice-filled glass. Top with soda.

GARNISH Orange wheel and a cherry.

GLASS Highball (300 mL).

Orgasm

Passionate Scene

(Australian)

45 mL	Suntory strawberry liqueur	9	/34
60 mL	Orange juice	12	/34
60 mL	Lemonade	12	/34
5 mL	Lemon juice	1	/34

1 barsp Passionfruit pulp
1 scoop Ice

METHOD Pour Suntory strawberry liqueur into a Highball glass and add a scoop of ice. Add orange and lemon juice, and then the lemonade. Top with passionfruit pulp. Do not stir.

GARNISH Orange wheel and strawberries. Straws.

GLASS Highball (300 mL).

Created by James Manuel David, Pacific International, Cairns. Winner ABG National Competition (Long Drink), 1986. Mixing this cocktail Mr David won the 'Efficiency Award' at the IBA World Cocktail-mixing Championship, Rome, 1987.

Paula Stafford

(Australian)

30 mL	Gordon's gin	1	/3
30 mL	Pimm's No 1 cup	1	/3
30 mL	Sabra	1	/3

1 piece Gold leaf
Ice

METHOD Place ingredients in a mixing glass, including a piece of gold leaf. Stir so that the gold leaf breaks up. Strain into glass.

GARNISH None.

GLASS Standard cocktail (140 mL).

Created by Sir Ian Orton, 1969.

Peach Daiquiri

(International)

30 mL	White rum	2	/5
30 mL	Peach liqueur	2	/5
15 mL	Lemon juice	1	/5

3 slices Peach
1/3 scoop Ice

METHOD Blend.

GARNISH Cherry.

GLASS Standard cocktail (140 mL).

Perfect Martini

See Martini, Perfect.

Pimm's

A Pimm's is an old-fashioned drink which becomes popular from time to time. Recipes usually suggest mixing Pimm's No 1 cup with soda, lemonade or dry ginger ale, but a combination of two of these can be used. The following is probably the most popular combination:

30 mL Pimm's No 1 cup
        Lemonade
        Dry ginger ale
        Ice

METHOD Half fill a large Highball glass or goblet with cubed ice. Pour the Pimm's over the ice. Fill the remainder of the glass with two-thirds lemonade, one-third dry ginger ale. Stir gently.

GARNISH Thin slice each of orange and lemon, a large slice of cucumber peel, sprig of mint (optional). Long straws.

GLASS Large Highball (420 mL) or goblet.

Pimm's

Pina Colada

There are several different recipes used in Australia for mixing Pina Coladas. Listed below are two of the most popular and a mocktail variation. In place of coconut cream you can use one of the proprietary brands of coconut rum, e.g. Malibu.

Pina Colada, No 1
(International)

45 mL	White rum	3	/10
75 mL	Pineapple juice	5	/10
30 mL	Coconut cream	2	/10

2 scoops Crushed ice

METHOD Blend (at high speed). Do not strain.

GARNISH Pineapple wedge and two cherries.

GLASS Colada (400 mL).

Pina Colada, No 2
(Australian)

30 mL	White rum	1	/6
30 mL	Coconut cream	1	/6
90 mL	Pineapple juice	3	/6
30 mL	Cream	1	/6

Pineapple pieces
Ice

METHOD Blend for about fifteen seconds.

GARNISH Pineapple wedge and a cherry. Long straw.

GLASS Colada (400 mL).

Pina Colada Mocktail
(Australian)

30 mL	Coconut cream	1	/6
90 mL	Pineapple juice	3	/6
30 mL	Lime cordial	1	/6
30 mL	Cream	1	/6

Half slice Fresh pineapple
Ice

METHOD Blend.

GARNISH Pineapple wedge with a cherry.

GLASS Colada (400 mL).

Pineapple Delight
(Mocktail)
(Australian)

60 mL	Pineapple juice	4	/5
15 mL	Grenadine	1	/5

Dry ginger ale
Ice

METHOD Build ice, pineapple juice and grenadine. Top with ginger ale.

GARNISH Two lemon wheels.

GLASS Highball (300 mL).

Pink Elephant
(Australian)

15 mL	Vodka	3	/23
15 mL	Galliano	3	/23
15 mL	Crème de noyeau	3	/23
15 mL	Orange juice	3	/23
15 mL	Grenadine	3	/23
40 mL	Cream	8	/23

Ice

METHOD Shake and strain.

GARNISH Sprinkle of cinnamon.

GLASS Standard cocktail (140 mL).

Created by Sir Ian Orton at the Pink Elephant Bar, Chevron Hotel, Surfers Paradise in 1966.

Pina Colada

Pink Lady
(International)

45 mL	Gin	3	/4
15 mL	Grenadine	1	/4
5 mL	Egg white (optional)		
	Ice		

METHOD Shake and strain.

GARNISH No garnish.

GLASS Martini (90 mL).

Pink Panther
(Australian)

30 mL	Pernod	1	/2
30 mL	Cointreau	1	/2
5 mL	Grenadine		
	Lemonade		
	Ice		

METHOD Build all ingredients except lemonade over ice. Top with lemonade.

GARNISH Strawberry.

GLASS Highball (300 mL).

Pink Pussy
(Australian)

30 mL	Campari	1	/2
30 mL	Peach liqueur	1	/2
1	Egg white		
5 mL	Bitter lemon		
	Ice		

METHOD Shake and strain all ingredients except bitter lemon into an ice-filled Highball glass. Top with bitter lemon.

GARNISH Whole slice of lime.

GLASS Highball (300 mL).

Planter's Punch, No 1
(International)

60 mL	Dark rum	6	/10
30 mL	Lemon or lime juice	3	/10
10 mL	Grenadine	1	/10
	Soda		
	Ice		

METHOD Build all ingredients except soda over ice. Top with soda.

GARNISH Slice of lemon or orange.

GLASS Balloon (285 mL).

Planter's Punch, No 2
(International)

60 mL	White rum	4	/10
15 mL	Orange curaçao	1	/10
15 mL	Maraschino	1	/10
30 mL	Lemon juice	2	/10
30 mL	Pineapple juice	2	/10
10 mL	Dark rum		
	Ice		

METHOD Build ingredients except dark rum over ice. Float dark rum on top.

GARNISH Half slice of pineapple and a cherry.

GLASS Highball (300 mL).

Poached Pear and Ginger Daiquiri
(Australian)

45 mL	Bacardi white rum	3	/8
30 mL	Monin ginger syrup	2	/8
45 mL	Lemon juice	3	/8
1	Fresh poached pear (small)		
	Ice		

METHOD Blend.

GARNISH Pear slice.

GLASS Tulip flute (180 ml).

From the Grand Pacific Blue Room, Sydney.

Planter's Punch

Portagaf

See glossary.

Porto Flip

(International)

45 mL	Port	3	/4
15 mL	Brandy	1	/4
1	Egg yolk		
	Ice		

METHOD Shake and strain.

GARNISH Grated nutmeg.

GLASS Standard cocktail (140 mL)

Prairie Oyster

(Pick-me-up)
(International)

10 mL	Worcestershire sauce	2	/5
10 mL	Tomato sauce	2	/5
5 mL	White vinegar	1	/5
1	Egg yolk (unbroken)		
	Salt and pepper (to taste)		

METHOD Pour the Worcester sauce and the tomato sauce into the glass. Stir. Gently add the unbroken egg yolk. Splash the vinegar over the top. Add salt and pepper to taste.

GARNISH No garnish.

GLASS Old Fashioned (180-240 mL).

NOTE The unfortunate victim (the hungover customer) is supposed to drink a Prairie Oyster at one gulp. If served with a beer chaser, the Prairie Oyster is called a Bush Oyster.

Pretty Woman

(Australian)

30 mL	Brown crème de cacao	2	/6
15 mL	Strawberry liqueur	1	/6
45 mL	Cream	3	/6
	Ice		

METHOD Shake and strain.

GARNISH Strawberry.

GLASS Standard cocktail (140 mL).

Pussyfoot

(Mocktail)
(International)

60 mL	Orange juice	1	/3
60 mL	Lemon juice	1	/3
60 mL	Lime juice	1	/3
1	Egg yolk		
	Ice		

METHOD Shake and strain.

GARNISH Slice of orange, slice of lemon, two long straws.

GLASS Highball (300 mL).

Q.F.

(Shooter)
(Australian)

15 mL	Kahlua	1	/3
15 mL	Midori melon liqueur	1	/3
15 mL	Bailey's Irish Cream	1	/3

METHOD Layer in the above order.

GARNISH No garnish.

GLASS Shot (60 mL).

Queensland Bulldog
(Australian)

15 mL	Bundaberg rum	1	/3
15 mL	Vodka	1	/3
15 mL	Kahlua	1	/3
20 mL	Milk		
20 mL	Cream		
5 mL	Coca-Cola		
	Ice		

METHOD Build all ingredients except
Coke over ice. Top with Coke.

GARNISH Orange wedge.

GLASS Highball (300 mL).

From Frankies Bar, Rydges Southbank, Brisbane.

Quick Comfort
(Shooter)
(Australian)

15 mL	Kahlua	1	/3
15 mL	Midori melon liqueur	1	/3
15 mL	Southern Comfort	1	/3

METHOD Layer in the above order.

GARNISH No garnish.

GLASS Shot (60 mL).

Redback Spider
(Mocktail)
(Australian)

30 mL	Raspberry cordial
2 tblsp	Ice-cream
7 mL	Cream (whipped)
	Lemonade

METHOD Place one tablespoon of ice-
cream in the glass. Add 10 mL of lemonade and the cordial. Blend carefully,
using a bar spoon. Top with lemonade.
Be very careful that the drink does not
foam over the rim. Add the second
tablespoon of ice-cream and top with
whipped cream.

GARNISH Two black straws.

GLASS Highball (300 mL).

Red Corvette
(Australian)

30 mL	Midori melon liqueur	1	/2
30 mL	Strawberry liqueur	1	/2
4	Strawberries		
	Crushed ice		

METHOD Blend to a semi-frappé with
two scoops of ice.

GARNISH Strawberry.

GLASS Standard cocktail (140 mL).

From the Boardwalk Bar, Wrest Point Casino, Hobart.

Red Eye
(Australian)

	Tomato juice
	Beer
1	Egg yolk

METHOD Fill glass with half tomato
juice and half beer. Float the yolk on
top.

GARNISH No garnish.

GLASS Highball (300 mL).

NOTE You can substitute non-alcoholic
beer for full strength beer to make a Red
Eye Mocktail.

Red Head
(Australian)

15 mL	Bacardi white rum	1	/6
30 mL	Blue curaçao	2	/6
30 mL	Cherry advocaat	2	/6
15 mL	Apricot nectar juice	1	/6
5 mL	Lemon juice		
	Ice		

METHOD Blend all ingredients except
advocaat. Float advocaat.

GARNISH Cherry.

GLASS Colada (400 mL).

NOTE For a creamy drink, use ice-
cream instead of ice.

From Redford's Bar, Carlton Crest Hotel, Brisbane.

Red Wine Cooler
(Australian)

90 mL	Red wine	6	/11
30 mL	White wine	2	/11
15 mL	Sugar syrup	1	/11
15 mL	Orange juice	1	/11
15 mL	Lemon juice	1	/11

Soda
Ice

METHOD Build over ice. Top with soda.

GARNISH Four lemon wheels.

GLASS Colada (400 mL).

Reflections
(Australian)

30 mL	Frangelico	4	/7
2 tblsp	White crème de cacao	2	/7
1 tblsp	Chéri-Suisse	1	/7

Ice

METHOD Stir and strain.

GARNISH Two maraschino cherries with stems. Cut half a centimetre off a red straw and use it to join the two cherry stems, by pushing the stems into one end of the straw. Arrange the cherries so that one is in the cocktail and the other outside, the one in the cocktail appearing to be a reflection of the one outside.

GLASS Martini (90 mL).

Created by Barry Emerson on the Gold Coast.

Rhett Butler
(Australian)

30 mL	Southern Comfort	2	/5
30 mL	Orange curaçao	2	/5
15 mL	Lemon juice	1	/5
5 mL	Lime cordial		

Soda
Ice

METHOD Build.

GARNISH Orange wheel and a cherry.

GLASS Highball (300 mL).

Rob Roy
(International)

45 mL	Scotch whisky	3	/5
30 mL	Sweet red vermouth	2	/5

3 drops Angostura bitters

Ice

METHOD Stir and strain.

GARNISH Maraschino cherry.

GLASS Martini (90 mL).

Rocket Fuel
(Australian)

15 mL	White rum	1	/4
15 mL	Vodka	1	/4
15 mL	Tequila	1	/4
15 mL	Gin	1	/4

Lemonade
Ice

METHOD Build spirits. Top with lemonade.

GARNISH Lemon wheel.

GLASS Highball (300 mL).

Rocky Road
(Australian)

30 mL	Frangelico	2	/9
15 mL	White crème de cacao	1	/9
15 mL	Cherry brandy	1	/9
75 mL	Cream	5	/9

Ice

METHOD Blend.

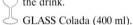

GARNISH Glass lined with strawberry topping and chocolate topping, strawberry first and chocolate second. Fresh strawberry and marshmallow on top of the drink.

GLASS Colada (400 ml).

From the Crown Entertainment Complex, Melbourne.

Roman Coffee
(International)

15 mL Galliano
       Coffee (piping hot)
       Cream (lightly whipped)

METHOD Sugar frost a champagne saucer (see Section 4 on Garnishes). Pour in the Galliano and ignite it. Twist the glass around at a 45° angle to caramelise the sugar. Immediately the sugar has caramelised pour in hot black coffee. (The glass will not crack.) Float lightly whipped cream on top, and serve.

GARNISH A small amount of Galliano can be whipped into the cream.

GLASS Champagne saucer.

NOTE It is usually unnecessary to add any sugar as the Galliano is very sweet.

See also Irish Coffee.

Rose
(International)

15 mL	Cherry brandy	1	/5
15 mL	Kirsch	1	/5
45 mL	Dry vermouth	3	/5

Ice

METHOD Stir and strain.

GARNISH Cherry.

GLASS Martini (90 mL).

Royal Fizz
(International)

30 mL	Gin	2	/5
30 mL	Lemon juice	2	/5
15 mL	Sugar syrup	1	/5

1	Egg
	Soda
	Ice

METHOD Shake and strain the gin, lemon juice, sugar syrup, and egg. Add two or three cubes of ice to the glass. Top with soda.

GARNISH Half strawberry.

GLASS Highball (300 mL).

NOTE Care has to be taken when adding the soda to make sure it does not FIZZ over the side!

R.S.A.
(Mocktail)
(Australian)

15 mL	Lime cordial	1	/2
15 mL	Lemon cordial	1	/2

| Lemonade |
| Dry ginger ale |
| Ice |

METHOD Build. Top with half lemonade and half dry ginger ale.

GARNISH Two lemon wheels in the drink.

GLASS Highball (300 mL).

Rum Punch

(International)

375 mL	Jamaica rum	15	/80
375 mL	White rum	15	/80
750 mL	Orange juice (unsweetened)	30	/80
300 mL	Pineapple juice (unsweetened)	12	/80
200 mL	Lime cordial	8	/80

20 drops   Angostura bitters
1 litre   Ice

METHOD Mix all ingredients in a punch-bowl with plenty of ice.

GARNISH Pineapple pieces, orange slices, lemon slices and mint.

GLASS Wine glass (240 mL).

SERVES Fifteen.

Russian Roulette

(Australian)

30 mL	Vodka	2	/4
15 mL	Galliano	1	/4
15 mL	Lemon juice	1	/4

Ice

METHOD Shake and strain.

GARNISH No garnish.

GLASS Martini (90 mL).

Rusty Nail

(International)

30 mL	Scotch whisky	1	/2
30 mL	Drambuie	1	/2

Ice

METHOD Fill the glass with ice. Build the ingredients. Stir.

GARNISH Twist of lemon (optional).

GLASS Old Fashioned (180-240 mL).

Rusty Russian

(Shooter)
(Australian)

15 mL	Kahlua	1	/3
15 mL	Scotch whisky	1	/3
15 mL	Drambuie	1	/3

METHOD Layer in the above order.

GARNISH No garnish.

GLASS Shot (60 mL).

Safe Sex

(Shooter)
(Australian)

15 mL	Strawberry liqueur	1	/3
15 mL	Bailey's Irish Cream	1	/3
15 mL	Cointreau	1	/3

METHOD Layer in the above order.

GARNISH No garnish.

GLASS Shot (60 mL).

Salty Dog

(International)

45 mL	Vodka	3	/10
105 mL	Grapefruit juice	7	/10

Ice

METHOD Salt the rim of the glass. Fill the glass with crushed ice. Add the vodka and grapefruit juice. Stir.

GARNISH Optional.

GLASS Highball (300 mL).

Samba
(Australian)

30 mL	Midori melon liqueur	2	/11
30 mL	Lena banana liqueur	2	/11
15 mL	Malibu	1	/11
60 mL	Pineapple juice	4	/11
30 mL	Cream	2	/11

Ice

METHOD Blend.

GARNISH Strawberry.

GLASS Colada (400 mL).

From Vivaz Restaurant, The Rocks, Sydney.

Sangria
(International)

90 mL	Red wine	6	/7
15 mL	Brandy	1	/7

Lemonade
Ice

METHOD Build wine and brandy. Top with lemonade.

GARNISH Lemon, orange and lime wheels.

GLASS Colada (400 mL).

Sax on the Beach
(Australian)

30 mL	Frangelico	2	/9
30 mL	Lena banana liqueur	2	/9
15 mL	Triple sec	1	/9
60 mL	Cream	4	/9

Fresh strawberries
Ice

METHOD Blend.

GARNISH Strawberry.

GLASS Flute (180 ml) (180 mL).

From Jazz n'Blues Bar, Brisbane City Travelodge.

Scottie was Beamed Up
(Australian)

15 mL	Galliano	1	/3
30 mL	Tequila	2	/3

Cubed ice

METHOD Build over cubed ice.

GARNISH Twist of lemon.

GLASS Old Fashioned (180-240 mL).

Screaming Lizard
(Shooter)
(Australian)

20 mL	Green Chartreuse	1	/2
20 mL	Tequila	1	/2

METHOD Layer in the above order.

GARNISH No garnish.

GLASS Shot (60 mL).

Screaming Multiple Orgasm
(Australian)

30 mL	Bailey's Irish Cream	2	/7
30 mL	Cointreau	2	/7
15 mL	Galliano	1	/7
30 mL	Cream	2	/7

Ice

METHOD Build.

GARNISH Cherries and strawberry.

GLASS Balloon (285 mL).

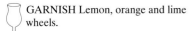

Screwdriver
(International)

30 mL Vodka
       Orange juice (fresh)
       Ice

METHOD Half fill the glass with cubed ice. Add vodka. Top with orange juice.

GARNISH Orange wheel or orange spiral. Two black straws.

GLASS Highball (300 mL).

Scud Missile
(Shooter)
(Australian)

15 mL	Kahlua	1	/3
15 mL	Bailey's Irish Cream	1	/3
15 mL	Malibu	1	/3

METHOD Layer in the above order.

GARNISH No garnish.

GLASS Shot (60 mL).

Sex in the Snow
(Shooter)
(Australian)

15 mL	Cointreau	1	/3
15 mL	Malibu	1	/3
15 mL	White sambuca	1	/3

METHOD Layer in the above order.

GARNISH No garnish.

GLASS Shot (60 mL).

Sex on the Beach
(Australian)

30 mL	Midori melon liqueur	2	/6
15 mL	Vodka	1	/6
15 mL	Strawberry liqueur	1	/6
30 mL	Pineapple juice	2	/6
5 mL	Grenadine		
	Ice		

METHOD Blend.

GARNISH Strawberry.

GLASS Standard cocktail (140 mL).

Sex on the Rocks
(Australian)

30 mL	Vodka	2	/5
15 mL	Kahlua	1	/5
15 mL	Grand Marnier	1	/5
15 mL	Bailey's Irish Cream	1	/5
	Milk		
	Ice		

METHOD Build spirit and liqueurs over ice. Top with milk.

GARNISH Half wheel of orange and a cherry.

GLASS Highball (300 mL).

Shampoo
(Champagne cocktail)
(Australian)

15 mL	Gin	3	/8
5 mL	Pernod	1	/8
5 mL	Blue curaçao	1	/8
15 mL	Lemon juice	3	/8
	Sparkling wine (méthode champenoise)		

METHOD Build gin, Pernod, blue curaçao and lemon juice. Top with sparkling wine.

GARNISH Twist of lemon.

GLASS Flute (180 mL).

Screwdriver

Shandy

See glossary.

Shirley Temple, No 1

(Mocktail)
(International)

15 mL Grenadine
       Dry ginger ale
       Ice

METHOD Build into an ice-filled glass, stirring gently.

GARNISH Cherries.

GLASS Highball (300 mL).

Shirley Temple, No 2

(Mocktail)
(Australian)

60 mL Pineapple juice   4   /5
15 mL Passionfruit pulp   1   /5

       Lemonade
       Ice

METHOD Fill the glass half full of ice. Add pineapple juice. Top with lemonade. Float passionfruit pulp on top.

GARNISH Pineapple wedge and a cherry.

GLASS Highball (300 mL).

Shit on Grass

(Shooter)
(Australian)

30 mL Green crème de menthe 6 /7
5 mL   Bailey's Irish Cream 1 /7

METHOD Layer.

GARNISH No garnish.

GLASS Shot (60 mL).

Sidecar

(International)

30 mL Brandy   6 /10
15 mL Cointreau   3 /10
5 mL   Lemon juice   1 /10

       Ice

METHOD Shake and strain.

GARNISH No garnish.

GLASS Martini (90 mL).

Siggi's Chocolate Sailor

(Australian)

15 mL Bailey's Irish Cream   1 /6
15 mL Frangelico   1 /6
15 mL Brown crème de cacao   1 /6
60 mL Cream   3 /6

Half   Fresh banana
       Ice

METHOD Blend.

GARNISH Strawberry and shaved chocolate.

GLASS Champagne saucer (180 mL).

From Siggi's Wine Bar, The Heritage, Brisbane.

Siggi's Fizz

(Australian)

30 mL Cointreau   1 /3
60 mL Orange juice (fresh) 2 /3

       Sparkling wine
       (méthode champenoise)

METHOD Build.

GARNISH Twist of orange.

GLASS Flute (180 mL).

From Siggi's Wine Bar, The Heritage, Brisbane.

Silver Fizz
(International)

30 mL	Gin	2	/5
30 mL	Lemon juice	2	/5
15 mL	Sugar syrup	1	/5
1	Egg white		
	Soda		
	Ice		

METHOD Shake and strain the gin, lemon juice, sugar syrup and the egg white. Add two or three cubes of ice to the glass. Top with soda.

GARNISH Long straws.

GLASS Highball (300 mL).

NOTE Care has to be taken when adding the soda or the drink may FIZZ over the side.

Singapore Sling
(International)

30 mL	Gin	3	/6
10 mL	Cherry brandy	1	/6
20 mL	Lemon juice	2	/6
	Soda		
	Ice		

METHOD Shake all the ingredients except the soda. Strain into an ice-filled glass. Stir in soda.

GARNISH Slice of lemon and a cherry.

GLASS Highball (300 mL).

Skull Candy
(Shooter)
(Australian)

10 mL	Midori melon liqueur	1	/6
10 mL	Suntory strawberry liqueur	1	/6
10 mL	White rum	1	/6
10 mL	Crème de cassis	1	/6
10 mL	Lemon juice	1	/6
10 mL	Triple sec	1	/6

METHOD Layer in the above order.

GARNISH No garnish.

GLASS Shot (60 mL).

Slippery Nipple
(Shooter)
(Australian)

30 mL	White sambuca	2	/3
15 mL	Bailey's Irish Cream	1	/3

METHOD Layer in the above order.

GARNISH No garnish.

GLASS Shot (60 mL).

Sloe Comfortable Screw
(International)

30 mL	Vodka	2	/4
15 mL	Sloe gin	1	/4
15 mL	Southern Comfort	1	/4
	Orange juice		
	Ice		

METHOD Build vodka, sloe gin and Southern Comfort into an ice-filled glass. Top with orange juice.

GARNISH Long straws.

GLASS Highball (300 mL).

See also Comfortable Screw and Long Sloe Comfortable Screw.

Snakebite
(Australian)

Half   Cider
Half   Beer
10 mL Crème de cassis

METHOD Build.

GARNISH No garnish.

GLASS Pilsner.

Snowball
(International)

30 mL Advocaat   6 /7
5 mL   Lime juice cordial 1 /7

       Lemonade
       Ice

METHOD Build over ice. Top with lemonade.

GARNISH Half slice of orange, two cherries.

GLASS Highball (300 mL).

Sober Brown Cow
(Mocktail)
(Australian)

30 mL Chocolate topping 2 /3
15 mL Coffee essence   1 /3

       Milk
       Ice

METHOD Build.

GARNISH Chocolate flakes.

GLASS Highball (300 mL).

Someplace Safe
(Mocktail)
(Australian)

One-third Large banana
5   Strawberries
Half   Kiwi fruit
60 mL   Cream
60 mL   Pineapple juice
5 mL   Grenadine
2 scoops   Ice

METHOD Blend all ingredients except grenadine. Pour into the glass. Add grenadine to finished drink.

GARNISH Pineapple and cherry wedge.

GLASS Colada (400 mL).

From Sheraton Towers Southgate, Melbourne.

Sours
See Whiskey Sour (note).

Southerly Buster
(Australian)

30 mL Brandy   2 /4
15 mL Dry vermouth 1 /4
15 mL Lime cordial 1 /4

       Dry ginger ale
       Ice

METHOD Build. Top with ginger ale.

GARNISH Long straws and a slice of lemon.

GLASS Highball (300 mL).

South Yarra Samurai
(Australian)

30 mL	Midori melon liqueur	1	/3
30 mL	Lena banana liqueur	1	/3
30 mL	Lemon juice	1	/3

Half   Large banana
1 scoop Ice

METHOD Blend.

GARNISH Strawberry in the glass.

GLASS Balloon (285 mL).

Spirit Sours
See Whiskey Sour (note).

Spring Sensation
(Australian)

30 mL	Midori melon liqueur	2	/5
15 mL	Cointreau	1	/5
15 mL	Lena banana liqueur	1	/5
15 mL	Lemon juice	1	/5

Crushed ice

METHOD Fill glass with crushed ice. Shake and strain.

GARNISH Spiral of lemon.

GLASS Martini (90 mL).

From the Sand Bar, Oasis Resort, Cairns, Queensland.

Spritzer
(International)

| Half | Dry white wine | 1 | /2 |
| Half | Soda | 1 | /2 |

METHOD Build over ice.

GARNISH Slice of lemon (optional).

GLASS Wine glass (240 mL).

Stinger
(International)

| 30 mL | Brandy | 2 | /3 |
| 15 mL | White crème de menthe | 1 | /3 |

Ice

METHOD Shake and strain or build into an ice-filled glass.

GARNISH No garnish.

GLASS Old Fashioned (180-240 mL) or standard cocktail (140 mL).

Strawberry Colada
(Australian)

30 mL	White rum	1	/7
30 mL	Coconut cream	1	/7
30 mL	Suntory strawberry liqueur	1	/7
90 mL	Pineapple juice	3	/7
30 mL	Cream	1	/7

4   Strawberries
1 scoop Ice

METHOD Place all ingredients in the blender and blend for about ten seconds.

GARNISH Strawberries, pineapple wedge.

GLASS Colada (400 mL).

Strawberry Colada Mocktail
(Australian)

30 mL	Coconut cream	1	/6
90 mL	Pineapple juice	3	/6
30 mL	Raspberry cordial	1	/6
30 mL	Cream	1	/6

4   Fresh strawberries
Ice

METHOD Blend.

GARNISH Pineapple wedge with a cherry.

GLASS Colada (400 mL).

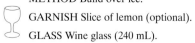

Strawberry Cloud
(Australian)

30 mL	Grand Marnier	2	/6
15 mL	Kahlua	1	/6
15 mL	Bailey's Irish Cream	1	/6
30 mL	Orange juice	2	/6

4	Strawberries
	Ice

METHOD Blend.

GARNISH No garnish.

GLASS Standard cocktail (140 mL).

From the City Hotel, Sydney.

Strawberry Daiquiri, No 1
(International)

30 mL	White rum	6	/10
15 mL	Strawberry liqueur	3	/10
5 mL	Lemon or lime juice	1	/10

3	Strawberries
Half scoop	Crushed ice

METHOD Blend all ingredients at high speed. Pour into glass unstrained.

GARNISH Fresh strawberry, two short straws.

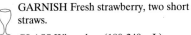

GLASS Wine glass (180-240 mL).

Strawberry Daiquiri, No 2
(Australian)

30 mL	White rum	2	/5
30 mL	Suntory strawberry liqueur	2	/5
15 mL	Lemon juice	1	/5

2-4	Strawberries
1/3 scoop	Ice

METHOD Blend. The consistency should be similar to that of a Frozen Daiquiri. Making a purée of the fruit in advance in anticipation of requests for the cocktail is often a good idea as it lessens the blending time. If the drink is blended for too long it will look watery.

GARNISH Half sugar-frosted strawberry.

GLASS Wine glass (240 mL).

NOTE Various fruit daiquiris can be made by changing the fruit and the liqueur. For example, a Mango Daiquiri is made by using a mango liqueur and a mango instead of strawberry liqueur and strawberries. Garnishes for fruit daiquiris are not set, but should be selected on the basis of appropriate colour and taste.

Strawberry Fizz
(International)

30 mL	Suntory strawberry liqueur	2	/5
30 mL	Lemon juice	2	/5
15 mL	Sugar syrup	1	/5

1	Egg white
3-4	Strawberries
	Soda
	Ice

METHOD Blend all ingredients except soda. Top with soda.

GARNISH Half strawberry.

GLASS Highball (300 mL).

Strawberry Daiquiri

Strawberry Margarita
(International)

30 mL	Tequila	2	/6
15 mL	Cointreau	1	/6
15 mL	Suntory strawberry		
	liqueur	1	/6
30 mL	Lemon juice	2	/6

5 mL	Egg white (optional)
2-4	Strawberries
	Ice

METHOD Blend.

GARNISH Salt frosted glass and half strawberry.

GLASS Standard cocktail (140 mL).

Strawberry Shortcake
(Australian)

30 mL	Suntory strawberry		
	liqueur	2	/8
15 mL	Malibu	1	/8
15 mL	White crème de cacao	1	/8
60 mL	Cream	4	/8

4-5	Strawberries
1 scoop	Ice

METHOD Blend.

GARNISH Grated chocolate.

GLASS Small balloon (285 mL).

Strawgasm
(Australian)

15 mL	Malibu	1	/9
15 mL	Strawberry liqueur	1	/9
15 mL	Galliano	1	/9
30 mL	Brown crème de cacao	3	/9
45 mL	Cream	3	/9

3	Strawberries
Quarter	Small banana
Half scoop	Ice

METHOD Blend.

GARNISH Chocolate-dipped strawberry.

GLASS Colada (400 mL).

Created by Mark Strobel. Winner of the 1992 Seagram's Student Cocktail Competition.

Summer Breeze
(Australian)

30 mL	Peach liqueur	1	/3
30 mL	Mango liqueur	1	/3
30 mL	Cream	1	/3

2 slices	Mango
1 tblsp	Passionfruit pulp
	Ice

METHOD Blend.

GARNISH Pineapple wedge and an orange wheel.

GLASS Highball (300 mL).

From Green Island Resort, Cairns, Queensland.

Summer Punch

(Australian)

375 mL	Vodka	3	/26
375 mL	Cointreau	3	/26
500 mL	Orange juice	4	/26
500 mL	Pineapple juice	4	/26
2 bottles	Sparkling wine	12	/26

2 punnets	Strawberries
4	Kiwi fruit
4	Passionfruit
1	Pineapple
	Ice

METHOD Wash and clean all the fruit.
Cut all the fruit into slices and wedges.
Place the fruit in a punch-bowl. Sprinkle
sugar over the fruit. Add the Cointreau
and leave overnight. Add the vodka,
sparkling wine and ice before serving.

GLASS Champagne saucer.

Sweet Martini

See Martini, Sweet.

Tequila Slammer

(International)

30 mL	Tequila	3	/5
20 mL	Dry ginger ale or		
	lemonade	2	/5

METHOD Build (neat).

GARNISH No garnish.

GLASS Shot (60 mL).

Down the hatch, slam the glass on the
bar!

Tequila Sunrise

(Long drink)
(Australian)

30 mL	Tequila	3	/4
10 mL	Grenadine	1	/4
	Orange juice		
	Ice		

METHOD Half fill the glass with ice.
Add the tequila. Top with orange juice.
Stir. Pour grenadine on top.

GARNISH Half slice of orange and a
cherry.

GLASS Highball (300 mL).

Created by Mike Elliot at the Chevron Hotel, Sydney
in the early 1960s.

Tequini

(Martini variation)
(International)

40 mL	Tequila	4	/5
10 mL	Dry vermouth	1	/5
	Ice		

METHOD Stir and strain.

GARNISH Twist of lemon.

GLASS Martini (90 mL).

Test-Tube Baby

(Shooter)
(Australian)

20 mL	Amaretto	1	/2
20 mL	Tequila	1	/2

2 drops Bailey's Irish Cream

METHOD Layer in the above order.

GARNISH No garnish.

GLASS Shot or test-tube (60 mL).

Tetanus Shot
(Shooter)
(Australian)

20 mL	Drambuie	1	/2
20 mL	Jack Daniel's whiskey	1	/2

METHOD Layer in the above order.

GARNISH No garnish.

GLASS Shot (60 mL).

The Loose Goose
See Loose Goose, The

The New Iced Tea
See New Iced Tea.

The Time Warp
See Time Warp, The

Tiki
(Australian)

30 mL	Vodka	1	/5
30 mL	Midori melon liqueur	1	/5
90 mL	Pineapple juice (fresh)	3	/5

Quarter Kiwi fruit
1 scoop Ice

METHOD Half fill the glass with ice.
Blend the ingredients and pour them
into the glass over the ice.

GARNISH Pineapple spear and a slice
of kiwi fruit.

GLASS Highball (300 mL).

Created by Sir Ian Orton.

Time Warp, The
(Australian)

20 mL	Midori	4	/13
20 mL	Malibu	4	/13
15 mL	Pineapple juice	3	/13
5 mL	Blue curaçao	1	/13
5 mL	Raspberry cordial	1	/13

Ice

METHOD Shake and strain the first
three ingredients. Add the blue curaçao
and raspberry cordial to the glass. Both
will sink.

GARNISH Cherry with lime rind legs in
the form of a spider.

GLASS Standard cocktail (140 mL).

Created by Brett Hutson. Winner of the 1993
Australian After-dinner Cocktail Championship.

Toddlezone, No 1[*]
(Australian)

30 mL	Frangelico	2	/9
15 mL	Bailey's Irish Cream	1	/9
15 mL	Kahlua	1	/9
75 mL	Cream	5	/9

10 mL   Honey
1 small scoop Ice

METHOD Blend. Dribble the honey
down the inside of the glass in four clear-
ly separate panels before adding the
ingredients.

GARNISH Honey-lined glass. Strawberry and chocolate flakes on top of the
drink.

GLASS Colada (400 mL).

From the Crown Entertainment Complex, Melbourne.

*NOTE: the word 'Toblerone' is a registered trade
mark and may not be used commercially as the name
of a cocktail.

Tom Collins

Toddlezone, No 2
(Australian)

30 mL	Bailey's Irish Cream	1	/3
30 mL	Frangelico	1	/3
30 mL	Cream	1	/3

1 tsp	Honey
	Ice

METHOD Blend.

GARNISH Shaved chocolate and toasted almonds.

GLASS Standard cocktail (140 mL).

From Horizons Bar, ANA Hotel, The Rocks, Sydney.

Toddlezone, No 3
(Shooter)
(Australian)

15 mL	Frangelico	1	/4
15 mL	Tia Maria	1	/4
15 mL	Cream	1	/4
15 mL	Honey	1	/4

METHOD Layer.

GARNISH No garnish.

GLASS Shot (60 mL).

Tom Collins/John Collins
(International)

30 mL	Gin	3	/6
20 mL	Lemon juice	2	/6
10 mL	Sugar syrup	1	/6

1 barsp	Castor sugar
	Soda
	Ice

METHOD Build lemon juice and sugar over ice. Stir. Add gin. Stir again. Top with soda. Stir gently.

GARNISH Whole slice of lemon on the rim of the glass. Two white straws.

GLASS Highball (300 mL).

See note (next column)

NOTE Sugar syrup can be used instead of castor sugar. A Tom Collins is normally a warm climate drink — long, cool and refreshing. John Collins is an alternative name for a Tom Collins.

VARIATIONS A Collins can be made with any spirit, but gin and whisky are most commonly used.

Traffic Light
(Shooter)
(Australian)

20 mL	Suntory strawberry liqueur	1	/3
20 mL	Lena banana liqueur	1	/3
20 mL	Midori melon liqueur	1	/3

METHOD Layer in the above order.

GARNISH No garnish.

GLASS Shot (60 mL).

NOTE The above Suntory products will achieve the desired layers. If you are using different brands you will have to experiment to achieve the traffic light effect.

Treasury Chest
(Mocktail)
(Australian)

30 mL	Coconut milk	1	/5
60 mL	Orange juice	2	/5
60 mL	Pineapple juice	2	/5

1 tblsp	Fruit salad
	Dry ginger ale
	Ice

METHOD Blend all ingredients except ginger ale. Top with ginger ale.

GARNISH Fresh pineapple or honey-dew melon.

GLASS Highball (300 mL).

From Conrad International Hotel and Treasury Bars, Brisbane.

Trinidad Fruit Punch
(Mocktail)
(International)

450 mL	Pineapple juice	5	/11
180 mL	Orange juice	2	/11
180 mL	Grenadine	2	/11
90 mL	Lime cordial	1	/11

5 mL	Angostura bitters
	Lemonade
	Ice

METHOD Mix all the ingredients except the ice and lemonade. Refrigerate. Fill a glass three-quarters full with ice. Half fill the glass with the mixture. Top up with lemonade.

GARNISH Pineapple wedge and a cherry. Short straws.

GLASS Old Fashioned (180-240 mL).

SERVES Twenty.

Tropical Field
(Australian)

30 mL	Seagram's strawberry liqueur	2	/7
15 mL	Seagram's cherry brandy	1	/7
30 mL	Pineapple juice	2	/7
30 mL	Cream	2	/7

| | Ice |

METHOD Shake and strain.

GARNISH Half strawberry and a cherry.

GLASS Standard cocktail (140 mL).

Created by Tok Wing Wong, 1988.

Tropical Fruit Cup
(Mocktail)
(Australian)

15 mL	Raspberry cordial	1	/7
45 mL	Orange juice	3	/7
30 mL	Pineapple juice	2	/7
15 mL	Lemon juice	1	/7

| | Lemonade |
| | Ice |

METHOD Half fill the glass with ice. Add the raspberry cordial, orange juice, pineapple juice and lemon juice. Top with lemonade. Stir.

GARNISH Pineapple wedge, cherry, slice of orange and strawberry, with a sprig of mint.

GLASS Colada (400 mL).

Tropical Sunset
(Mocktail)
(Australian)

60 mL	Pineapple juice	6	/13
60 mL	Orange juice	6	/13
10 mL	Lemon juice	1	/13

4	Strawberries
Half	Banana
2 slices	Mango
5 mL	Grenadine
1 tblsp	Passionfruit
	Ice

METHOD Blend all ingredients except grenadine and passionfruit. Gently pour grenadine through. Float passionfruit.

GARNISH Pineapple wedge, strawberry.

GLASS Colada (400 mL).

From Kani's on the Esplanade, Cairns, Queensland.

Turkish Delight
(Australian)

30 mL	Sabra	2	/13
15 mL	Parfait Amour	1	/13
30 mL	Cream	2	/13
120 mL	Milk (full cream)	8	/13
5 mL	Grenadine		
	Ice		

METHOD Chill glass. Coat inside of chilled glass with a dash of grenadine. Stand glass on its rim. Shake and strain.

 GARNISH Chocolate flakes.

GLASS Colada (400 mL).

Created by David Cook, 1989.

Velvet Hammer
(International)

30 mL	Cointreau	1	/3
30 mL	Kahlua	1	/3
30 mL	Cream	1	/3
	Ice		

METHOD Shake and strain,

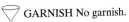 GARNISH No garnish.

GLASS Standard cocktail (140 mL).

Vibrator
(Shooter)
(Australian)

15 mL	Bailey's Irish Cream	1	/3
15 mL	Lena banana liqueur	1	/3
15 mL	Malibu	1	/3

METHOD Layer in the above order.

GARNISH No garnish.

GLASS Shot (60 mL).

Virgin Barman
(Australian)

30 mL	Malibu	2	/5
15 mL	Advocaat	1	/5
15 mL	Cherry advocaat	1	/5
15 mL	Blackberry Nip	1	/5
Quarter	Banana		
3	Strawberries		
150 mL	Pineapple juice		
	Ice		

METHOD Blend.

GARNISH Pineapple wedge.

GLASS Colada (400 mL).

From Market Buffet Restaurant, Wrest Point Casino, Hobart.

Virgin Mary

See Bloody Mary (note).

Vodkatini
(Martini variation)
(International)

40 mL	Vodka	4	/5
10 mL	Dry vermouth	1	/5
	Ice		

METHOD Stir and strain. Fill a mixing glass two-thirds full with ice. Pour in the ingredients. Stir gently for about ten seconds until the ingredients are cold. Strain into a chilled cocktail glass.

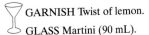 GARNISH Twist of lemon.

GLASS Martini (90 mL).

Vodkatini

Volcanic Eruption
(Australian)

30 mL	Kahlua	1	/3
30 mL	Opal Nera	1	/3
30 mL	Bailey's Irish Cream	1	/3

METHOD Layer.

 GARNISH No garnish.

GLASS Standard cocktail (140 mL).

Created by Nigel Frawley, 1992.

Voodoo
(Australian)

15 mL	Frangelico	1	/6
15 mL	Strawberry liqueur	1	/6
30 mL	Cream	2	/6
15 mL	Midori	1	/6
15 mL	Opal Nera	1	/6

Ice

METHOD Shake and strain the first three ingredients into the glass. Add the Midori and Opal Nera. Both will sink.

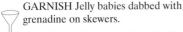 GARNISH Jelly babies dabbed with grenadine on skewers.

GLASS Standard cocktail (140 mL).

Created by Eric Woolford, 1993.

West Indies Yellow Bird
(Australian)

30 mL	White rum	2	/10
15 mL	Lena banana liqueur	1	/10
15 mL	Galliano	1	/10
30 mL	Lemon juice	2	/10
30 mL	Orange juice	2	/10
30 mL	Pineapple juice	2	/10

1¹/₂ scoops Ice

METHOD Blend.

 GARNISH Pineapple wedge with cherry.

GLASS Balloon (570 mL).

Wet Dream
(Shooter) (Australian)

15 mL	Kahlua	1	/3
15 mL	Bailey's Irish Cream	1	/3
15 mL	Tequila	1	/3

METHOD Layer in the above order.

GARNISH No garnish.

GLASS Shot (60 mL).

Wet Spot
(Australian)

30 mL	Midori	2	/7
15 mL	Frangelico	1	/7
30 mL	Apple juice	2	/7
30 mL	Cream	2	/7
30 mL	Passionfruit pulp (to float)		

Ice

METHOD Shake and strain.

GARNISH Passionfruit pulp float, pineapple wedge with cherry.

GLASS Standard cocktail (140 mL).

Created by Tracy Phelan, 1993.

Whiskey Highball
(International)

30 mL	Rye whiskey	1	/5
120 mL	Dry ginger ale	4	/5

3 drops Angostura bitters (optional)
Ice

METHOD Half fill the glass with ice. Add the whiskey and the drops of Angostura bitters. Top with dry ginger ale.

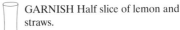 GARNISH Half slice of lemon and straws.

GLASS Highball (300 mL).

NOTE Soda can be substituted for ginger ale.

Whiskey Sour
(International)

30 mL	Bourbon whiskey	2	/5
30 mL	Lemon juice	2	/5
15 mL	Sugar syrup	1	/5
5 mL	Egg white		
	Ice		

METHOD Shake and strain.

GARNISH Lemon wedge and a cherry.

GLASS Standard cocktail (140 mL) or small wine glass (140-200 mL).

NOTE Any style of whiskey can be used, although bourbon or Canadian is recommended. The style of the whiskey used will dramatically affect the taste of the drink. As the name implies, the cocktail is usually deliberately sour, but the proportions of the ingredients can be altered for customers who prefer a sweeter drink.

Different spirits and liqueurs can be substituted for whiskey to make other sours. For example, substitute brandy for whiskey to make a Brandy Sour, or Amaretto di Saronno to make an Amaretto Sour.

White Lady
(International)

30 mL	Gin	6	/10
15 mL	Cointreau	3	/10
5 mL	Lemon juice	1	/10
5 mL	Egg white (optional)		
	Ice		

METHOD Shake and strain.

GARNISH Cherry.

GLASS Martini (90 mL).

White Russian
(International)

45 mL	Vodka	9	/19
30 mL	Kahlua	6	/19
20 mL	Cream	4	/19
	Ice		

METHOD Build Kahlua and vodka into ice-filled glass. Float cream on top by pouring it over the back of a bar spoon. Do not stir.

GARNISH No garnish.

GLASS Old Fashioned (180-240 mL).

White Spider
(International)

| 30 mL | White crème de menthe | 1 | /2 |
| 30 mL | Vodka | 1 | /2 |

METHOD Build over ice.

GARNISH No garnish.

GLASS Old Fashioned (180-240 mL).

Wild Orchard
(Australian)

15 mL	Advocaat	3	/21
30 mL	White crème de cacao	6	/21
15 mL	Monin strawberry syrup	3	/21
20 mL	Orange juice	4	/21
20 mL	Cream	4	/21
5 mL	Lemon juice	1	/21
	Ice		

METHOD Build advocaat. Blend other ingredients and build over.

GARNISH Raspberry purée.

GLASS Standard cocktail (140 mL).

From the Pacific Vista Hotel, West Hobart, Tasmania.

Wild Strawberry
(Australian)

30 mL	White crème de cacao	2	/8
30 mL	Strawberry liqueur	2	/8
15 mL	Galliano	1	/8
30 mL	Orange juice	2	/8
15 mL	Coconut cream	1	/8

4   Fresh strawberries
Half scoop   Ice

METHOD Blend.

GARNISH Strawberry and chocolate flakes.

GLASS Tulip flute (180 mL).

Willie Swayer
(Australian)

30 mL	Bailey's Irish Cream	2	/7
15 mL	Kahlua	1	/7
15 mL	Lena banana liqueur	1	/7
45 mL	Cream	3	/7

Half   Fresh banana
       Chocolate syrup
       Ice

METHOD Swirl chocolate syrup in glass, then blend all other ingredients.

GARNISH Slice of banana, half strawberry.

GLASS Colada (400 mL).

From Willie McBride's Restaurant, Cairns, Queensland.

XYZ
(International)

30 mL	Golden rum	2	/4
15 mL	Cointreau	1	/4
15 mL	Lemon juice	1	/4

Ice

METHOD Shake and strain.

GARNISH Cherry.

GLASS Martini (90 mL).

Yellow Bird
See West Indies Yellow Bird.

Yellow Fever
(Australian)

30 mL	De Kuyper Peachtree Liqueur	2	/6
15 mL	Bénédictine	1	/6
45 mL	Orange juice	3	/6

5 mL   Egg white
Quarter Peach
1 scoop Ice

METHOD Blend.

GARNISH Strawberry and whole lime slice on rim.

GLASS Tulip flute (180 mL).

Created by James O'Donnell, 1987.

Whiskey Sour

Zombie
(International)

30 mL	Light rum	2	/13
30 mL	Golden rum	2	/13
30 mL	Dark rum	2	/13
30 mL	Lemon juice	2	/13
30 mL	Pineapple juice	2	/13
30 mL	Apricot nectar	2	/13
15 mL	Overproof rum	1	/13
5 mL	Sugar syrup		
	Ice		

METHOD Fill a glass three-quarters full with ice. Shake and strain all ingredients except the overproof rum into the glass. Gently pour the overproof rum on top.

GARNISH Pineapple spear, mint, orange slice, and a cherry.

GLASS Large Highball (450 mL).

Zulu Warrior
(Australian)

30 mL	Midori melon liqueur	1	/3
30 mL	Suntory strawberry liqueur	1	/3
30 mL	Lemon juice	1	/3
1 slice	Rockmelon		
3	Strawberries		
1½ scoops	Ice		

METHOD Blend.

GARNISH Slice of rockmelon.

GLASS Balloon (285 mL).

Created by Michael Chapman, 1986.

3 Coffee

Espresso coffee is served in most modern bars and the ability to make a good coffee is therefore an essential bartending skill.

To make a good coffee you need:

1. A clean machine.
2. Milk that is fresh, cold and suitable. It is best to use one of the many brands of reduced-fat milk now available.
3. Freshly-ground coffee. (It is important that the grind is correct; if in doubt discuss this with your supplier.)

Points to remember when using espresso machines:

1. The standard portion (dose) of coffee is approximately seven grams (7g).
2. All coffee made in an espresso machine should have a thick creamy head, called the crema. Over extraction is indicated by the crema being lighter in colour.

Espresso/short black

A black coffee served in a small glass or demitasse. A standard portion (dose) of approximately 7g of coffee is required to make a short black.

Long black

A black coffee served in a regular-size glass or cup.

Cappuccino

A serving of espresso topped with hot milk and foam. The ideal cappuccino consists of one-third espresso coffee, one-third milk, and one-third foam. The foam should be thick, creamy, and long-lasting, not a light froth which quickly dissipates. A coffee stain should be noticeable around the edge of the foam. The colour of the stain indicates the strength of the cappuccino.

A sprinkled garnish of powdered chocolate or cocoa is expected by Australian customers.

Flat white/café au lait

A 'long' white coffee made with equal quantities of milk and coffee (i.e. less milk than a caffè latte). The milk should be hot but not frothed. The French term, *café au lait* means 'coffee with milk'.

Mocha

A caffè mocha is a mixed drink of espresso coffee, chocolate, and milk. Place a scoop of chocolate powder in the cup and then fill the cup with an espresso coffee, milk, and foam, as if making an ordinary cappuccino.

Caffè latte

Usually served in a glass, a caffè latte (Italian for 'milk coffee') is a milky light-brown coffee with a collar of froth or foam on top. The ideal caffè latte consists of one-third espresso coffee and two-thirds hot milk.

Macchiato

A serving of espresso 'stained' *(macchiato)* with either a small quantity of cold milk, or hot milk.

Iced coffee

Using a tall glass, add ice cubes, 30mL espresso coffee, sugar if required, and chilled milk. Stir. Garnish with a scoop of vanilla ice-cream and a sprinkle of chocolate shavings.

Hot chocolate

In a cup or mug, mix chocolate powder and a dash of hot milk. Add hot frothed milk. Garnish with a sprinkle of powdered chocolate. A marshmallow in the drink is optional.

Vienna coffee

A long black espresso coffee topped with whipped cream and a sprinkling of chocolate.

4 Garnishes

G ARNISHES are increasingly important to modern cocktail presentation, particularly to the long drink cocktails which are especially popular in Australia because of our relatively warm often semi-tropical climate.

Strictly speaking a garnish is edible (a piece of fruit for example) while a decoration (e.g. a swizzle stick) is not.

Selection and preparation of fruit

Bars frequently purchase second-grade fruit for use in garnishes. If this is done (and we do not recommend it) it is most important that the fruit with the fewest blemishes should be used for garnishes and the rest to make juices.

All the fruit used for garnishes should be carefully washed. It can then be put on display to improve the bar's appearance. For example fruit can be taken from an attractive display of polished lemons to make spirals and twists of peel. When the peel has been used the fruit should be squeezed to make lemon juice.

Before opening the bar prepare a sufficient quantity and variety of garnishes, and store any surplus under refrigeration. Try to prepare sufficient garnish, but only sufficient, to last until the end of your shift. Don't waste fruit by preparing too much.

Garnishes should be handled whenever possible not with your hands but with tongs or other appropriate implements. Use sharp knives to cut the fruit; blunt knives are more likely to cause an accident. Never cut fruit on the bar counter; always use a clean cutting board. At the end of trading hours all remaining fresh garnishes should be covered with plastic wrap and then refrigerated for use on the next day's trading. Covering garnishes will make them last longer in a fresh and appealing condition.

How a particular cocktail is decorated and garnished is very much a matter of individual decision, but with the cocktail recipes in this book we do suggest appropriate or standard garnishes for each of them.

A cocktail garnish should be attractive for its main function is to please the eye, which invariably pleases the palate. Edible garnishes also impart some flavour to the drink.

If you decide to create your own garnish for a cocktail be careful not to overdo it. Don't hide the drink under a jungle of fruit salad so that the drinker needs a machete to cut a way through to the drink itself. Overdone garnishes both look ludicrous and are expensive to make.

Never re-use a garnish once it has been served. This rule applies no less to cocktail umbrellas, plastic animals, swizzle sticks and other inedible decorations than it does to fruit garnishes.

The following pages show the method of making the standard garnishes:

1 Olive on a toothpick
2 Cherry on a toothpick
3 Twist of lemon
4 Lemon (or orange) spiral
5 Sprinkle of nutmeg
6 Lemon wheel
7 Orange wheel
8 Half a strawberry
9 Lemon wedge
10 Stick of celery
11 Cucumber rind
12 Half slice of orange (or lemon) with cherry
13 Sugar-frosted strawberry
14 Sugar or salt-frosted glass
15 Harlequin frosting
16 Frappé with cherry
17 Kiwi fruit wheel with cherry
18 Pineapple and cherry
19 Pineapple wedge with cherry.

1
Olive on a toothpick

1   Impale a stoned olive on a toothpick.

2   Place it in the glass.

Martini

2
Cherry on a toothpick

1   Impale a cherry on a toothpick.

2   Place it in the glass.

Manhattan

3
Twist of lemon

1 Select and wash a crisp-skinned lemon. Cut off a very thin slice of peel.

2 Twist the slice of peel over the drink so that the juice (oil) from the peel floats on top of the liquid.

3 Drop the twist of lemon peel into the glass.

Vodkatini

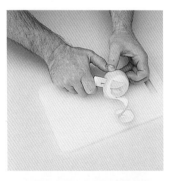

4
Lemon (or orange) spiral

1 Take a whole clean lemon (or orange) and, using a sharp paring knife or a citrus peeler, cut the spirals. If you are using a knife, care must be taken to pare off only the skin of the fruit with as little of the white as possible.

2 Place the spiral in the glass, hooking the starting end of the spiral over the rim.

Horse's Neck

5
Sprinkle of nutmeg

1 Grate a fresh nutmeg.

2 Sprinkle the grated nutmeg on top of
   the cocktail.

Brandy Alexander

6
Lemon wheel

1 Select and clean a lemon.

2 Using a sharp knife, cut the lemon into slices approximately half a centimetre thick. Make sure the slices are cut evenly.

3 Cut each slice from the centre to the outside peel.

4 When it is needed, place the lemon wheel on the rim of the glass. If it has been cut correctly the slice will fit firmly on the rim of the glass.

Tom Collins

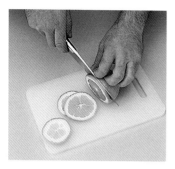

7
Orange wheel

1 Select and clean an orange.

2 Using a sharp knife, cut the orange into slices half a centimetre thick, cutting the slices as evenly as possible.

3 Cut each slice from the centre to the outside peel.

4 When needed, place the slice on the rim of the glass. If it has been cut correctly the slice will fit firmly on the rim of the glass.

Screwdriver

8
Half a strawberry

1 Select and wash premium quality strawberries.

2 Cut selected strawberries in half from the leaf to the tip.

3 Make a slice in each strawberry about half a centimetre from the cut edge.

4 When required place a half strawberry on the rim of the glass.

Strawberry Daiquiri

9
Lemon wedge

1 Select and clean a lemon. Top and tail it
  (cut off both its ends).
2 Stand the lemon with one end on the
  cutting board. Cut it into wedges.

3 Cut the wedges under the peel deep
  enough for them to be held firmly on
  the rim of the glass.
4 A cherry on a toothpick can be added to
  the wedge if required.

5 When needed, place a wedge on the rim
  of the glass.

Whiskey Sour

10
Stick of celery

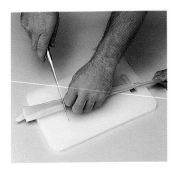

1   Select and wash a stick of celery.
    Cut off and retain about 18-20 cms of
    the leaf end of the celery stick. Send the
    rest of the stick to the kitchen.

2   Trim the leaf end of the celery to the
    shape required.

3   Place in the glass.

Bloody Mary

11
Cucumber rind

1   Select and wash a cucumber.

2   With a sharp paring knife slice off a slice of the rind (skin) about 12 cms long and thick enough to include a little of the white flesh. (The flesh adds to the flavour and keeps the rind firm.)

3   Place in the glass.

Pimm's

12
Half slice of orange (or lemon) with cherry

1 Select and clean a lemon or orange and top and tail the fruit (cut off both its ends).

2 Stand the fruit on end on the cutting board. (This technique reduces the risk of the fruit slipping.) Cut the fruit in half.

3 Lay each half flat on the cutting board and cut it into slices about half a centimetre thick.

4 Impale the cherry on a toothpick and then push the toothpick into a slice of the fruit through the peel.

5 Place the garnish in the glass or balance it with the rim of the glass under the cherry.

Harvey Wallbanger

13
Sugar-frosted strawberry

1 Select and wash premium quality
   strawberries.

2 Make a slice about 1 cm deep into the
   end of a strawberry.

3 Dip half the strawberry (the sliced end
   first) into lemon juice.

4 Roll the sliced end of the strawberry in
   sugar, ensuring an even coating of sugar.

5 Slide the strawberry onto the rim of a
   glass.

Golden Dream

14
Sugar or salt-frosted glass

1 Cut a whole lemon in half.

2 Cut a nick half a centimetre deep into the flesh of the fruit.

3 Place the rim of the glass into the nick in the lemon. Twist the glass round until the whole rim has been evenly moistened with the juice of the lemon.

4 Holding the base of the glass, place the rim into a saucer filled with sugar (or salt). Ensure an even distribution of the frosting.

Brandy Crusta

15
Harlequin frosting

1   Arrange instant coffee and sugar in a saucer in alternate quarters.

2   Moisten the rim of the glass with lemon juice by twisting the glass round in a nick cut into half a lemon.

3   Holding the base of the glass, place the rim into the centre of the saucer so that it is frosted with four equal quarters of coffee and sugar.

Harlequin

16
Frappé with cherry

1   Fill the glass with finely crushed ice.

2   Add a measure of the liqueur.

3   Place a cherry on top.

Crème de Menthe Frappé

17
Kiwi fruit wheel with cherry

1   Select a firm-skinned kiwi fruit.
    Cut off the end.

2   Cut the fruit into slices about half a
    centimetre thick. If the slices are thinner
    they may not stand firmly on the glass.
    Make a slice in the kiwi fruit from the
    centre core to the outer rim.

3   Impale a cherry on a toothpick.

4   Press the toothpick into the kiwi fruit
    through the skin from the side opposite
    the slice.

5   Place the kiwi fruit wheel on the rim of
    the glass.

Australia III

18
Pineapple and cherry

1 Top and tail the pineapple, leaving some of the leaves intact.

2 Stand the pineapple on end on the cutting board and cut it in half.

3 Slice the halves lengthwise into slices about 1 cm thick.

4 Cut the slices in half, and retain the top half of the slice with some leaves.

5 Make a cut near to and parallel with the core edge of the slice.

6 Impale a cherry on a toothpick and push the toothpick into the slice.

7 Slide the slice of pineapple onto the glass.

Planter's Punch

19
Pineapple wedge with cherry

1   Top and tail the pineapple.

2   Stand the pineapple on the cutting board and cut it in half.

3   Lay half the pineapple flat on the cutting board and cut it into slices 1 cm thick.

4   Cut the slices into wedges.

5   Impale a cherry on a toothpick and push the toothpick into the curved skin edge of the wedge.

6   Slice each wedge from the point to the skin.

7   Slide the wedge of pineapple onto the edge of the glass.

Pina Colada

5 Ice

Ice is an essential element in almost all mixed drinks. It is important to have plenty of it available and to handle it correctly so that it does not excessively dilute the drinks it is in.

When using a shaker or a mixing glass make sure that it is filled two-thirds full of ice, so that the liquids and other substances being mixed are brought down to the same temperature as the ice as quickly as possible. Strangely enough, the more ice that is used, the less the ice melts and dilutes the drink. As the ice melts it absorbs heat from the surrounding substances, that is the drink being mixed, until it is the same temperature. So, the more the ice, the more quickly it will absorb the heat from the drink, and when the ice and the drink are nearly the same temperature the ice will melt only very slowly. When shakers and mixing glasses are filled two-thirds full of ice, only 15-20 per cent of the ice will melt and dilute the drink.

A plentiful supply of ice is essential in any bar. Most bars will have easy access to an ice machine on the premises. Ice machines are not normally found in the bar itself as they generate too much noise and heat.

Make plenty of ice in the ice machine and store it in a container or bin which allows the melted ice to drain away and not 'wet' the remainder. The best kind of container is a sink or something similar, with a drainage hole. The container should be restocked with ice regularly throughout trading hours so that a plentiful supply of fresh ice is always available.

Crushed ice is used rarely behind the bar, except in an ice bucket when used for cooling bottles of wine; for most mixing purposes cubed ice should be used.

When dispensing ice, use an ice scoop, tongs, or a slotted spoon (see Section 10.6 on Equipment). Do not use your fingers or another glass.

⑥ Syrups and mixes

1 Sugar syrup

Sugar syrup, often called gomme syrup, is used for sweetening drinks.

To make sugar syrup

1   Fill a jug thee-quarters full with white sugar.
2   Add just sufficient boiling water to be able to stir the mixture of sugar and water.
3   Stir the mixture until its consistency resembles honey.
4   Allow the mixture to settle.
5   Pour the clear liquid into a bottle or decanter, and label it.

2 Bloody Mary Mix

Bloody Mary mix can be prepared before trading in bars that serve large numbers of Bloody Mary cocktails. It has the advantages of speed and consistent quality.

To make Bloody Mary mix:

600 mL	Tomato juice	10	/11
60 mL	Lemon juice	1	/11
8 drops	Tabasco sauce		
20-30 mL	Worcestershire sauce		
	Salt and pepper (to taste)		

3 Sour Mix

Sour mixes, like Bloody Mary mixes, can be pre-prepared for use in busy bars. Sour mixes are used in Daiquiris, Fizzes, Margaritas and Sours.

To make Sour mix:

600 mL	Lemon juice	6	/10
300 mL	Sugar syrup	3	/10
100 mL	Egg white	1	/10

7 Mixing drinks and mixing terms

Mixing terms

Cocktail mixing has its own specialist terminology. Here is a list of some of the commonly-used terms with explanations of the processes involved:

- ### Shake and strain
Fill the cocktail shaker two-thirds full with ice. Pour in the ingredients. Shake vigorously, using a short, snappy action, holding the shaker above the shoulder. Using a Hawthorne strainer strain the cocktail into the correct glass.

- ### Stir and strain
Fill a mixing glass two-thirds full with ice. Pour in the ingredients. Stir until cold. Strain, using a Hawthorne strainer, into the correct glass.

- ### Blend
Blended ingredients are mixed in a blender. Place the required amount of ice in the blender and then add the ingredients. Blend until the required consistency is achieved. This usually takes about ten seconds, more or less, depending on the ingredients and how many cocktails are being mixed in the blender. After blending pour all the contents of the blender unstrained into the glass. Be sure to see that an ice-crushing blade is fixed to the blender.

- ### Build
To build a drink is to mix it in the glass without any pre-mixing. Built drinks are usually served with swizzle sticks and straws.
    There is a sequence to follow when building a mixed drink in a glass:
1 Select the appropriate clean glass.
2 Place ice in the glass.
3 Add the alcohol (for example, gin).
4 Add the mixer (for example, tonic water).
5 Garnish (for example, with a twist of lemon).

▪ Float

Floating is the term used to describe the placing of one liquid above the rest of the ingredients so that it does not mix with them in the glass but 'floats' on top. For example, cream is 'floated' on top of the coffee in an Irish coffee.

▪ Layer

When ingredients are layered they are built carefully one on top of the other so that they remain in distinct layers in the glass.

▪ Muddle

To muddle ingredients is to crush them together in the bottom of the glass with a glass 'muddler' or the back of a bar spoon. See Old Fashioned No. 1 and Mint Julep.

▪ Dash

A 'dash' is an inexact term sometimes used to describe the quantity of an ingredient released in a quick spurt from a bottle equipped with a speed pourer—about 5 mL.

▪ Neat

Drinks are served as 'neat' or 'plain' if they are straight from the bottle without ice, water, or a mixer.

▪ On-the-rocks

A drink served on-the-rocks is served with a large quantity of cubed ice. Simply pour the drink (usually a spirit like Scotch) over the ice in the glass.

▪ Straight up

Served with no ice; neat.

▪ Shooters

Traditionally (in cold-climate countries) a glass of liquor taken neat prior to having a beer, in Australia the term 'shooter' has come to mean a layered cocktail without ice similar to a pousse-café, and often 'skulled'.

Tips on Mixing

Accuracy
Consistent accuracy in measurement ensures a desirable uniformity in mixed drinks. Follow all recipes carefully.

Carbonated ingredients
Add these last to maintain maximum fizz.

Customers' recipes
Regardless of the recipe usually used in your bar, if a customer requests that a drink be made to his or her own specifications, do exactly what is requested. The right way to make a drink is the way the customer likes it.

Pouring more than one drink
When pouring two or more blended or shaken drinks, do not fill the first glass before pouring some of the drink into the second. Fill all the glasses at the same time, pouring a little at a time into each glass, to ensure that all the glasses have the same proportions of froth and the other ingredients.

Shaking cocktails
When shaking a cocktail, don't rock it to sleep. A short, sharp, snappy action is best.

Spirits and water
When serving a spirit with water, as for example in a Scotch-and-water, always ask the customer exactly how much water to add. Tastes vary considerably. A simple 'Will you say "when", Madam?' will suffice.

⑧ Measures

Throughout this book we have used metric measurements, that is volumes in millilitres (mL). The standard measure for drinks in Australia is 30 mL.

Accurate measures

The importance of accurate measures cannot be over-emphasized. Far too many bartenders are unable to make the same drink consistently because they lack pouring judgement. This can only result in customer dissatisfaction. Follow all recipes carefully and pour them accurately.

Free pouring

Only the most experienced bartenders should attempt to free-pour measures of spirit or liqueur; however other ingredients, such as juices, cream, soft drinks and milk, are usually free-poured.

Learning to free-pour accurate measures is an essential bartending skill. The only way to acquire this skill is through practice and experience. During preparation time free pouring can be practised, using water, and then checked for accuracy.

Measuring spirits

Most of the main spirits and some liqueurs are measured electronically or with mechanical measures. These are described in Section 10 on Equipment. See also Section 7 on Mixing Drinks.

9 Mise-en-place

Mise-en-place is a French term which means, literally, 'put-in-place' or, more loosely but more helpfully, 'everything in place'. It is the term used to describe the process of getting everything ready in the kitchen as well as the bar. The bartender, as well as attending to all the preparatory tasks outlined in Section 13 on Bar Duties, must see that the bar is stocked not only with all the necessary spirits, liqueurs, etc. but with a wide range of other items, such as juices, cherries, and olives which are used for mixers or as garnishes, etc.

Listed below are some of the essential items which should be stocked:

FRESH FRUIT (IN SEASON), JUICE, AND DAIRY PRODUCTS

Bananas
Cantaloupe or rockmelon
Celery
Cream
Cucumber
Eggs (whites and yolks)
Kiwi fruit
Mangoes
Milk
Mint
Lemons
Lemon juice
Oranges
Pineapple
Strawberries

CANNED FRUIT AND JUICES

Cherries
Cocktail onions
Grapefruit juice
Olives
Orange juice
Pineapple juice
Tomato juice

SUNDRY ITEMS

Angostura bitters
Chocolate flakes
Cinnamon
Grenadine
Lemon cordial
Lime cordial
Nutmeg
Parasols
Pepper
Raspberry cordial
Salt
Straws (long and short)
Sugar
Sugar cubes
Sugar syrup
Swizzle sticks
Tabasco sauce
Toothpicks
Worcestershire sauce.

All these items, both processed and fresh, must be stored correctly. All juices and fruit should be kept covered, preferably under a plastic wrap and in the refrigerator. Juices and milk deteriorate quickly if they are not kept covered and cool.

10 Equipment

1 Pourers and measures

a Standard spirit measures (30 and 15 mL)

Throughout Australia the standard measure is 30 mL and so 15 mL is a half measure (as used for example for a half brandy and ginger ale). The measure is designed primarily for use with the five basic spirits—brandy, gin, rum, vodka and whisky—but it can be used to measure any liquid. The conical shape (when inverted) allows the spirits to drain off so that the measure can be used repeatedly with different spirits without their tastes affecting each other. However, with particularly aromatic spirits like ouzo, and with sticky liquids like fruit juice, the measure must be washed clean after each use. The measure must be filled to the brim.

b Speed pourers

Speed pourers are not measures; they simply control and direct the flow of the liquid but they do not govern the quantity. They are most often used by experienced bartenders in cocktail bars who can judge measures by eye and who often require different quantities of various ingredients not necessarily in standard measures, in order to mix cocktails.

c Optic measure (30 mL)

This measure automatically refills after each drink has been poured, and the customer and bartender can see for themselves that the measure is full before a drink is poured. It is obtainable in both 15 and 30 mL measures.

d Posi-pour spirit measure

This is a more recent arrival than the optic measure. It is cheaper and less bulky and could in outward appearance be mistaken for a speed pourer. Posi-pours are available in a number of different measures.

e Emu measure

Emu measures are permanently fixed and electronically controlled to give 15 or 30 mL measures. They can be installed in batteries of up to 24 and programmed to show the number of measures poured. They are used for the basic spirits in bars, and are easy to use and accurate but bulky and relatively expensive. 'Emu'* is a brand name; other brands are available.

*EMU stands for Electronic Measuring Unit.

2 Cocktail shakers and strainers

a Standard shaker

The standard stainless steel cocktail shaker has an inbuilt strainer. The ingredients are placed in the base (ice first), the strainer is inserted and covered by the lid. When the cocktail has been shaken the lid is removed and the cocktail is poured through the strainer. This can be a fairly slow process, particularly for thicker creamy cocktails, and for that reason the standard cocktail shaker tends to be used in bars where relatively few cocktails are made. The strainer section can be removed after shaking, and a Hawthorne strainer inserted and used instead. This will increase speed.

b Hawthorne strainer

The Hawthorne strainer is in two parts, the frame and the wire coil. The coil must be removed and rinsed separately after straining cocktails which contain citrus fruit juices, as particles of the fruit catch in the wire. The protruding prongs are meant to balance on the rim of a cocktail shaker or mixing glass. The strainer (inserted in half of the cocktail shaker) should be held firmly in one hand and the liquid should pour out between the protruding prongs. Control over the flow of the liquid can be governed by the movement of the strainer on top of the cocktail shaker.

c Standard Boston shaker

The Boston shaker has two equal halves. The ingredients are poured into one half (ice first); the other half is inserted, and the cocktail shaken. Use a Hawthorne strainer to pour the cocktail.

d American-style Boston shaker

One half of the strainer is a mixing glass (see photograph opposite).

3 Mixing equipment

a   Mixing glass

This can be the glass half of the American-style Boston shaker, or a separately bought mixing glass. It is simply a heavy strong glass (about 500 mL). It is used for mixing cocktails with a clear liquids like Martinis or Manhattans, using a stir-and-strain technique. Pour through a Hawthorne strainer.

b   Mixing jug

A jug with a handle can be used instead of a plain mixing glass for stir-and-strain cocktails.

c   Hawthorne strainer

See previous page (10.2)

4 Openers

a Waiter's friend (2)
This basic tool has three parts: a knife, a worm (corkscrew) and a lever.

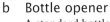

b Bottle opener
A standard bottle and can opener essential in any bar.

c Sparkling wine cork remover
This can be useful for stubborn corks which cannot easily be removed by hand. It is used as a lever under the lip of the cork.

5 Blender, ice bucket & water jug

a Blender

Several varieties of electric blender are available. This one is a Semak Vitamizer, a heavy-duty commercial blender with a stainless steel top. Domestic blenders with glass or plastic tops are not usually strong enough for use in professional bars. Blenders are used instead of shakers for cocktails using fruit, ice or when particular cocktails need to be made in bulk. It is useful to have several tops for use with the same base so that different tops can be used for the most popular cocktails and the top does not have to be carefully washed each time a different cocktail is asked for.

b Ice bucket

This is used for keeping chilled wine cold and is often kept in a stand by a dining table. Fill the bucket half to two-thirds full with a combination of ice (preferably crushed ice) and chilled water so that the bottle will stand in the bucket with the ice and water all round it.

c Water jugs

Jugs are available in a variety of sizes and shapes, some clear and some opaque. If jugs are kept in a refrigerator to chill the water, cover them in plastic wrap to keep the water free of any smells there may be.

6 Cutting board and equipment

a   Cutting board

The cutting board should be made of heavy plastic material, not wood. Wooden boards are unhygienic and are prohibited by health regulations.

b   Ice scoop

c   Tongs

Tongs are used for garnishes and for fruit which should not be touched by hand.

d   Bar spoon

The bar spoon is used for stir-and-strain cocktails.

e   Slotted spoon

The slotted spoon, like the ice scoop, is used to serve ice.

f   Knives (2)

Knives with permanently-sharp serrated edges are preferable.

g   Citrus zester

h   Citrus peeler

i   Melon-ballers

These are sometimes called parisienne cutters. They are used for garnishing.

⑪ Glasses

Choice of glassware

In the hospitality industry presentation is a major factor in generating sales, and it is as important for the bartender as it is for the chef. The appearance of drinks and the style in which they are presented is extremely important. Obviously, then, it is essential to have and to use the correct glassware.

Glassware is expensive and great care must be taken in its selection so that it is not only correct and attractive but can stand the inevitable wear and tear of use in the bar with a minimum of breakage. If your glassware is too fragile, or it is for some other reason inappropriate (if, for example, it is unstable in the glass baskets or trays), unnecessary breakages are inevitable and too much of the bar's potential profit will be lost simply because of the cost of replacing damaged or broken glassware.

Glass-washing machines

There is a large choice of industrial glass-washing machines. Before a particular machine is chosen the following points about washing glasses should be considered, as they will help ensure that, after washing, your glasses are left sparkling clean. Some machines may be more suitable for your needs than others.

a   Hot final rinse. Choose a machine with a hot final rinse. If the cycle finishes with a cold rinse the glasses will dry with streaky marks on them. Although machines with hot rinses at the end of the cycle take a little longer to cool they are much more likely to leave the glasses dry and sparkling clean.

b   Correct detergent injection. Use the correct detergent, and make certain that it is continually topped up. Don't try to guess the dilution of the detergent mixture. Too strong a solution will not rinse off properly and drinks served in the glasses will taste soapy. Too weak a solution, on the other hand, will not clean the glasses properly.

c   Sorting glassware. If you sort your glassware before washing it you will save a lot of time. Many bars keep out a number of baskets, one for each type of glass, and fill them simultaneously. When the bartender has filled a basket with dirty glasses of a particular type it is put through the washing machine and an empty basket for glasses of that type is put out to be loaded with dirty glasses. Routines like this enable the bar to work as efficiently as possible and reduce clutter in the working area.

d   Beer glasses require special attention especially in bars which serve food. They should be washed by hand on a specially-designed glass washing brush as well as in a glass washing machine. The brush should be in a sink filled with hot water and detergent. Only after the dirty glasses have been plunged several times over the brush should they be placed in a glass basket to go into the washing machine.

These duties are best performed in quiet periods during the afternoon, that is in the lull after lunch service, as well as after closing in the evening.

The following pages describe the types of glasses found in a professional bar, and the purposes for which they are used.

There are many types and varieties of glasses in use in bars around the country. Glassware is subject to fashion trends and it is impossible to feature all available glassware. In this section the intention is to depict a range of popular glassware currently in use. This is by no means the total range of available glassware.

When mixing drinks and cocktails it is important to use a glass that will hold the contents of the particular drink being prepared. The glasses depicted in the recipe section are a guide and in most cases they are the standard glass used by the bartenders for that particular drink. It is important to remember that famous quote, 'Everything is set in custard'. A recommendation is not a rule.

1 Cocktail glasses

a   Martini glass (90 mL)

This is used for stir-and-strain cocktails such as Manhattans and Martinis. Shapes vary. This was once the standard cocktail glass but it is now used less frequently; the trend is to use a larger glass in its place.

b   Standard cocktail glass (140 mL)

This glass is now used for most cocktails. It is the workhorse glass of the cocktail bar. It used to be thought of as a double cocktail glass, but it is now standard.

c   'Epsom' glass (140 mL)

This is an example of an alternative shape of glass for standard cocktails. It can also be used for sparkling wine.

d   Colada glass (400 mL)

One of the many varieties of large capacity tulip-shaped cocktail glasses. It is used for a variety of mixed drinks, for example Pina Coladas and Tropical Fruit Cups.

2 Mixed drinks glasses

a   Old Fashioned glass (180-240 mL)

Glasses of this type are usual for short mixed drinks consisting of a standard spirit and a mixer, for example brandy-and-dry. It is also used for Scotch on-the-rocks or Scotch, ice, and water but not for neat spirits which are usually served in a small wine glass. Old Fashioned glasses also suit drinks with no spirit base such as vermouth and ice, or Campari on-the-rocks.

Traditional Old Fashioned glasses have thick bottoms because the technique of making an Old Fashioned demands a strong glass to stand the pressure of muddling the sugar in the glass.

b   On-the-Rocks glass (180-240 mL)

This popular variety of the Old Fashioned, is so named because the shape of the glass reflects the chunkiness of the ice cubes in drinks served on-the-rocks.

c   Highball glass (300 mL)

Highball glasses are used for long drinks, which are popular in hot weather. Long drinks such as Highballs are good thirst-quenchers because the alcohol is diluted in the high proportion of non-alcoholic mixers. Cocktails served in Highball glasses usually have more elaborate garnishes.

3 Beer glasses

The names of beer glasses are very confusing because different terms are used in different States, and even in different parts of the larger States. The same term may mean different things in different States. On the other hand, the capacity of draught beer glasses is controlled by State liquor laws, We have therefore organized the draught beer glasses by capacity rather than by name. The illustration shows only a selection of the many common beer glasses.

a 200 mL standard beer glass

In Victoria and WA this is usually called simply 'a glass'; in NSW and NT it is called a Seven, and in SA it is called a Butcher.

b 285 mL draught beer glass

This glass is called a Middy in NSW and WA, a Pot in Victoria, Qld, and Tas, and a Schooner in SA.

c Pilsner glass (200 mL+)

This glass is used for bottled beer. Pilsner is a type of lager beer similar to that brewed at Pilsen (Plzen) in the Czech Republic, but the glass is suitable for use with all types of Australian beer.

d Beer goblet (200-285 mL)

Like the Pilsner glass, the beer goblet is used for bottled beer when the size of the glass is not controlled by Government regulation. The stem has the practical advantage that the beer is not warmed by the heat of the drinker's hand.

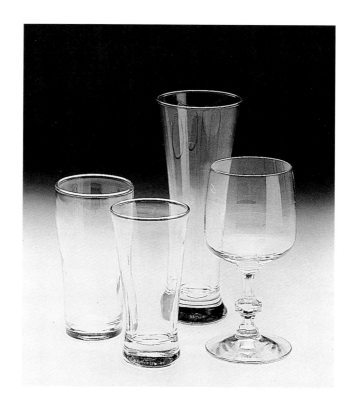

4 Sparkling wine glasses

a   Saucer
This is the traditional glass for serving sparkling wine. It is nowadays seldom used for that purpose and it is far less popular than the flute. However the saucer is often used for cocktails in place of the standard 140 mL cocktail glass.

b   Flute
The flute is the usual glass for sparkling wine. The narrow mouth helps to retain the sparkle and it allows the drinker to nose the wine and enjoy the bouquet. A disadvantage of the flute is that it is relatively difficult to wash and breakages can be high.

c   Tulip flute
This is a variation of the flute. Unlike the standard flute, the tulip flute is frequently used as a cocktail glass.

5 Wine glasses

a   **Sherry or port glass (60-90 mL)**
Traditionally sherry glasses had longer stems than port glasses but nowadays most bars use the same glass for both drinks. The glass also suits other fortified wines like muscat and madeira.

b   **Standard 180 mL wine glass**
Wine glasses come in a great variety of shapes and sizes. The smaller standard wine glass is usually used for white wine. Wine glasses are tending to get bigger with narrower mouths. They are not filled more than two-thirds full to allow the drinker room to nose the bouquet of the wine.

c   **Standard 240 mL wine glass**
The larger standard wine glass is usually used for red wines. Establishments which use only one type of wine glass use the bigger glass for both red and white wine. Wine glasses are normally used for wine coolers.

6 Brandy and liqueur glasses

a Liqueur glass (30 mL)

This 'Elgin' glass is the most commonly used glass for serving liqueurs.

b Shot glass (60 mL)

The shot glass is used for neat spirits customarily drunk in a single gulp like aquavit, Tequila Slammers, neat vodka or whisky chasers. It is also used for shooters.

The glass is also often used as a measure when cocktails are being mixed in bulk.

c Brandy balloon

Also known as snifters or brandy inhalers, brandy balloons are used for good quality brandies, especially cognacs and very old Australian brandies which the drinker will want to savour. The balloon shape is designed to fit the hand so that the brandy is naturally warmed by the drinker's body heat. The narrow mouth concentrates the bouquet.

Many cocktails are served in brandy balloons. Sizes vary from 285 mL to 600 mL.

12 The Bartender

What it takes

The professional bartender must be a great deal more than a dispenser of drinks. He or she must, of course, know the business and the commodities which are for sale. The bartender is responsible for the bar and its equipment—and sometimes for the cellar and storeroom as well. They must be kept clean, attractive, hygienic and safe. The bartender also has to deal face to face with the customers, and to do that well must be an expert, a psychologist, a salesperson, a performer, and a host.

This book is essentially about cocktails and how to make them, but let us never forget the one vital element over which neither the bartender nor the owner of the bar has any control, and on whom both are dependent—the customer.

The customer

Call him what you will: guest, customer, client—he or she is by far the most important person in any bar or any place where drinks are sold. A bar may be beautifully decorated, have huge stocks of the finest products, and have a bartender able to make any drink to perfection, but all will come to nothing unless the customer gets satisfaction when he patronizes the bar. Satisfying the customer is the all-important part of the bartender's duty. If the customer is satisfied all will probably be well; if he is dissatisfied everything else is useless.

Customers are human beings. They are people with the same feelings as the rest of us. The bartender must treat them as he or she would like to be treated. Greet them. Be welcoming and cheerful. Learn their names if possible. Attend to them promptly; nothing can ever be more important. Be polite. Treat them fairly. Admit fault; never argue with a customer. Know your bar and what you can offer. Help your customers to choose—the bartender is a salesperson and should sell by suggestion.

Your customers are your guests and they pay your wages. Every one of them is a VIP, and the bartender's profession is to serve them and make sure that they will want to return.

Customer service equals •presentation •liking people •being quick-minded •having high tolerance to customers and •valuing service.

13 Bar duties

The duties of a professional bartender go well beyond acting as a sales-person and serving drinks to customers. We list here the duties that are often expected of bartenders, though, naturally, not all of them will apply in all establishments all of the time.

Preparatory tasks

1   Clean and polish the bar and dispensing equipment.
2   Position tables, chairs, and ash-trays correctly.
3   Put out clean linen.
4   Check the bottled and keg beer supply and turn on the instantaneous beer-cooler.
5   Check and replenish stocks.
6   Check arrangements for the disposal of empty glasses.
7   Check that amusement machines are ready to play.
8   Check ventilation of the bar and service area.
9   Collect the float and prepare the till.
10 Prepare and put out bar sundries, such as fruit and nuts.
11 Prepare the mise-en-place for cocktail garnishing and service.
12 Prepare the glasswasher for use and check its detergent level.
13 Make a final check that the bar is ready for service.

Service and general tasks

1   Keep the working surfaces clean.
2   Maintain personal hygiene at a satisfactory level (see Section 14).
3   Reduce the number of safety hazards around the bar.
4   Dispense and price drinks.
5   Take cash for goods sold.
6   Check deliveries and requisitions.
7   Replenish supplies, keeping stocks to agreed stock levels, and assist in the operation of the stock control system.
8   Recognize and report unusually heavy demand for particular commodities.
9   Collect dirty glasses.
10 Wash glassware by hand and by machine.
11 Serve drinks at tables.
12 Serve meals when required.

13 Handle both draught and bottled beer supplies.
14 Clean and maintain the beer reticulation system.
15 Ensure stock (especially beer stock) rotation.
16 Wear protective clothing when appropriate.
17 Keep equipment and bar and storage areas clean.
18 Report stolen property.
19 Inform employer of shortages and breakages.

Closing tasks

1 Flush and close down the beer dispensing equipment.
2 Sort and return empty glassware.
3 Deal with dirty linen.
4 Deal with dirty ashtrays.
5 Clean up any bar games.
6 Clean dirty surfaces.
7 Attend to cash registers.
8 Cover and store any perishable goods.
9 Remove all rubbish.
10 Turn off the electrical and refrigeration equipment where necessary.
11 Make a final check that all equipment is clean and safely stored in its proper place, and that everything is as it should be.

14 Hygiene

The bartender and the bar and its equipment must at all times be kept perfectly clean. This is partly a matter of safety and public health, but it is also, and very importantly, one of the things which is absolutely essential for customer satisfaction.

Personal hygiene

Remember the following rules:
1   Uniforms should always be freshly laundered and pressed.
2   Hair should be clean, well-groomed, and off the face.
3   Make-up and jewellery should be used sparingly.
4   Fingernails should be kept clean and short.
5   Deodorant should be used.
6   Clean and comfortable shoes should be worn.
7   Protective clothing should be worn when preparing for service and when doing such jobs as stocking refrigerators and preparing garnishes.
8   A shower may be needed after heavy lifting (for example after cellar work).

Cleaning the bar

The following rules apply:
1   Bar surfaces and tables must be kept scrupulously clean and tidy at all times.
2   All surfaces must be cleaned repeatedly while the bar is open with the appropriate cleaning agent.
3   All bottles should be cleaned daily with a damp cloth.
4   Floors should be cleaned regularly to prevent accidents and to satisfy Health Department regulations.
5   Cupboards, refrigerators, glass racks, glass chillers and drip trays should be cleaned regularly and frequently.

Bar hygiene

Bar hygiene is no less essential than personal hygiene. It protects the staff as well as the customers. Note the following:

1 Never wash ashtrays in the dishwasher. Ashtrays must always be washed separately in the sink.
2 Always use lint-free disposable cloths when polishing glasses.
3 Wash your hands frequently especially after using a tissue or a handkerchief to blow your nose, after using the toilet, or after cleaning ashtrays.
4 Always remove all rubbish from the bar at the close of trading.
5 Never re-use the same glass for a customer's drinks.
6 Never smoke behind the bar.
7 Never eat behind the bar.

⑮ Tips for the bartender

▪ Bar lay-out

Lay out your bar to make it as attractive as possible to the eye and at the same time efficient for you to work in. Then make sure it stays that way always, returning bottles and equipment to their correct positions after use.

▪ Citrus fruit

When cutting up oranges, lemons and limes for use in drinks, cut away as much of the white membrane as possible and do not include it in the drink.

▪ Cocktails last (except for draught beer)

When a variety of drinks has been ordered by a customer always mix the cocktails last so they can be presented as freshly and as attractively as possible. But draught beer should be pulled last, after mixing cocktails.

▪ Drinking

Drinking behind the bar is a matter of management policy, but it is usually unacceptable.

▪ Effervescent (carbonated) ingredients

Never put sparkling or effervescent ingredients into a blender, cocktail shaker or mixing glass. Add carbonated ingredients to mixed drinks last to maintain maximum fizz.

▪ Filling glasses

Never fill glasses to the brim—it will only result in spillage and unnecessary cleaning up. Over-filled glasses are difficult to drink from and it is difficult to serve them.

▪ Fresh fruit juices

You can extract considerably more juice from citrus fruits if they are not refrigerated before they are squeezed. Some bartenders microwave the fruit for a few seconds before squeezing them as this makes it possible to extract even more juice.

▪ Handling glasses

Handle all glasses by their stems or bases to avoid smears.

▪ Ingredients

Use only good quality ingredients. Cocktails are usually delicate in flavour, and poor quality ingredients are often noticeable, spoiling their taste.

▪ Quiet moments

The pace of service in a bar can be likened to the action of waves. A bartender is often busy for ten minutes and then quiet for five. It is during these lulls that the professional bartender will prepare for the next wave of customers. This involves:

1 Replenishing stocks
2 Replacing empty spirit bottles
3 Cleaning ashtrays
4 Cleaning bar surfaces
5 Washing and sorting glassware
6 Removing rubbish from the bar
7 Replenishing the float (change) in the cash register.

▪ Smoking

Never smoke when on duty behind the bar. It is always unsightly and in some States it is illegal.

▪ Spilled drinks and unsatisfactory products

If your management policy is to replace spilled drinks or products customers are dissatisfied with, replace them immediately without query or comment other than an apology.

▪ Standing cocktails

Cocktails should not be kept standing. Mix them for immediate consumption. Cocktails, if allowed to stand after mixing, tend to separate.

▪ Substituting brands

The practice of substituting cheaper and relatively unknown brands for established products should be treated with great caution. It can easily result in customer dissatisfaction. Before using new or cheaper ingredients make sure that they are just as good as the established products. If a customer makes a specific request serve precisely what has been asked for. For example, if you are asked for a 'Bacardi and Coke' serve exactly that, and do not substitute some other white rum and another brand of cola.

▪ Telephone calls

When an outside call for a customer is received in the bar, always ask your customer if he or she wishes to speak with the caller before handing the phone over. Ask the caller to hold while you check whether your customer wishes to take the call.

16 Alcoholic strengths

Alcoholic strengths have traditionally been measured by three different scales:

1 The Sikes scale which was formerly used in Britain and the Commonwealth.
2 The Gay-Lussac (GL) scale which originated in France and became the standard scale in continental Europe.
3 The American scale used in the United States.

Naturally enough, misunderstandings between these scales have been many and frequent. Fortunately the situation has improved because the Sikes scale has become obsolete. In 1983 Britain adopted the Gay-Lussac scale which is now standard throughout the European Union, and most of the Commonwealth countries, including Australia, have adopted it also. However, the United States continues to use the traditional American scale.

All three scales operate on the same basic system. Pure water, containing no alcohol, is at the bottom of the scale and is rated 0° and pure (or absolute) alcohol is at the top of the scale. The top of the scale (for absolute alcohol) is, however, given a different numerical rating on the three scales. Absolute alcohol is 100° on the Gay-Lussac scale, 200° on the American scale, and was 175° on the old Sikes scale. The result was that the same alcoholic strength could be given a very different value on the three scales. For example, 40° GL (the strength of most normal spirits) is the same as 80° US proof, and 70° proof on the Sikes scale.

Alcohol by volume

Note that the Gay-Lussac (GL) scale, ranging from 0° GL for no alcohol, to 100° GL for absolute alcohol, is in fact just a way of expressing the level of alcohol as a percentage of the total volume of the liquid: 40° GL is the same as 40% alcohol by volume. The strength of all Australian and European alcoholic beverages is measured on this percentage of alcohol by volume basis, and is usually noted as such, i.e. '40% alc/vol' rather than '40° GL'.

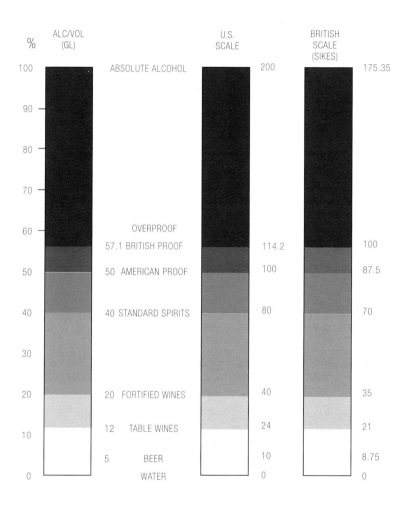

Proof spirits

Before modern scientific methods of testing the alcoholic content of distilled spirits were developed, spirits were tested or 'proved' by crude methods to make sure they had not been fraudulently diluted below a reasonable strength. A spirit was of 'proof' strength when a mixture of the undiluted spirit and water was just so sufficiently alcoholic that, when it was used to dampen gunpowder, the mixture would still burn explosively. The term 'proof spirit' remained in use long after accurate methods of measuring alcoholic strength had been developed. Both the Sikes and American scales retained the concept of 'proof' spirits. 'Proof spirit' (or 100° proof in the Sikes scale) was 57.1 % alc/vol and is 50% alc/vol in the American scale. In Australia we still occasionally use the term 'overproof', particularly when referring to very strong rum, to indicate a spirit of more than 100° proof on the old Sikes scale, i.e. stronger than 57.1% alc/vol.

Strengths of different beverages

Different brands of beverages have different strengths, but this is an approximate guide:

Low-alcohol beer	0.9% alc/vol
Light beer	3% alc/vol
Beer	5% alc/vol
Table wine	9-14% alc/vol
Fortified wine	17-22% alc/vol
Spirits	40% alc/vol
Overproof rum	58% alc/vol

The strength of liqueurs varies enormously. The traditional liqueurs like Drambuie or Grand Marnier are as alcoholic as spirits or even stronger (40% alc/vol or more), but nowadays many liqueurs are often little more alcoholic than some fortified wines (20-30% alc/vol).

⓱ Responsible Service of Alcohol (R.S.A.)

Since the early 1970s we have seen major changes in the service of alcohol. Governments have encouraged the Responsible Service of Alcohol at home and on licensed premises. This shift has been in response to changing community attitudes relating to the consumption of alcohol. A number of Government initiatives have encouraged if not compelled servers of alcohol to behave responsibly. These include:

1   The majority of States/Territories adopting the Blood Alcohol Concentration (B.A.C.) of .05 as the legal limit for driving.
2   Increased police testing for drink drivers.
3   Highly successful media advertising.
4   Training of hospitality employers and employees.
5   Licensing authorities discouraging:
    Happy hours
    Shooters
    Lay-backs
    Slammers
    Any other forms of quick alcohol consumption.

Responsible Service of Alcohol is not a flavour of the month issue; it is here to stay. To embrace the philosophy of R.S.A. in the home and in the hospitality industry we must change our focus on alcohol. We must adopt a formal policy for the Responsible Service of Alcohol for the following reasons:

1   To satisfy obligations imposed by licensing authorities.
2   To make your establishment more pleasant for staff and customers.
3   To avoid court action through injury caused by intoxicated customers.
4   To keep customers coming back to your establishment.

House Policy on R.S.A.

Governments through the licensing authorities are encouraging servers of alcohol to adopt a House Policy that reflects Responsible Service of Alcohol. At the moment this is a voluntary Code of Conduct that the majority of alcohol servers have adopted. An effective House Policy should contain these guidelines.

1 Do not serve alcohol to customers under the legal age.
2 Limit the number of customers on your premises to the licensed number. Do not overcrowd.
3 Do not serve intoxicated customers. Do not allow customers to become intoxicated on your premises.
4 Have a definite House Policy that defines how to deal with intoxicated customers. Staff must be trained to put the policy into practice.
5 Promote food, especially snack-type meals.
6 Encourage a nominated driver policy. That is, offer the nominated driver non-alcoholic beverages. Some establishments offer these free to the nominated driver.
7 Make it easy for customers to access taxis.
8 Promote non-alcoholic and low alcoholic beverages.
9 Keep up with current training and policy on R.S.A.

If your House Policy on R.S.A. is to be successful it must become part of the organization's culture. Staff and management must be proactive in enforcing the House Policy.

Even on the domestic scene society is demanding that we observe the principles of Responsible Service of Alcohol. It is not responsible to allow our relatives and friends to leave our homes intoxicated and drive a car.

In this edition of *The Australian Bartender's Guide to Cocktails* we have given recipes for a much larger number of mocktails or non alcoholic cocktails than in previous editions. Non-alcoholic cocktails require the same skills to prepare as alcoholic cocktails. Mocktails are more interesting to prepare and consume than the alternative soft drinks. They can be reasonably inexpensive to prepare and yield a high profit margin. Mocktails are becoming very popular especially at lunch times when customers have to return to work.

Intoxication

To help prevent customers from becoming intoxicated we need to understand some basic facts.

Identifying the intoxicated customer

As a rule customers should only be served alcohol if they can:

1 Stand up unassisted.
2 Speak without a slur.
3 Walk to and from the bar without swaying.
4 Can order the drink.
5 Can efficiently produce the payment.
6 Can carry the order away from the bar.
7 Behave in a manner that is not loud or offensive to other customers.

While looking for these signs of intoxication, you must be aware of the possibility that your customer is not intoxicated but may suffer from some physical disability. It is against the law to discriminate against people by refusing service on the grounds of their disability.

Becoming intoxicated

You will all be aware that some people can drink more than others and seem as if they are not intoxicated. Some only need to consume a small amount of alcohol to become intoxicated.

We become intoxicated and cannot perform the above tasks if:

1 We drink too much too fast.
2 We have an empty stomach.

Other factors which will contribute to becoming intoxicated are build, sex, and level of body fat.

Generally more than two standard drinks in the first hour and one standard drink every hour after that will give a man a blood alcohol concentration (B.A.C.) greater than 0.05%. (Most women will reach a B.A.C. of 0.05% after consuming fewer standard drinks than most men.) This formula can only be used as a guide because not all beers, wines and spirits are equally strong. Some examples of typical standard drinks are given in the chart below.

Standard drinks

These are all 'standard drinks'.

Light beer
1 can
375 mL

Regular beer
1 glass
200 mL

Table wine
1 small glass
100 mL

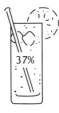

Port or sherry
1 small glass
60 mL

Mixed drinks
1 glass
30 mL of spirits
plus mixer

Spirits
1 measure
30 mL

18 The Australian Bartenders Guild

The Australian Bartenders Guild was formed in 1962. It is a non-union non-profit making organization; its aim is to encourage professional excellence among bartenders.

The ABG promotes the interests of the trade in which its members are engaged by raising professional standards and by assisting in the training of bartenders.

The Guild also encourages the creation of new Australian cocktails and mixed drinks by organizing competitions, by recording the successful recipes and by giving publicity to them. It also organizes for its members other events such as lectures, visits to breweries, and social gatherings and dinners.

The ABG is one of the 34 national bartenders organizations which are affiliated to the International Bartenders Association, (IBA). The headquarters of the IBA moves between the member organizations and is not permanently fixed in one country.

The competitions organized by the ABG are conducted under the rules of the IBA. Every year competitions are arranged to select the winners of State Titles and the winners go forward to compete for the Australian Titles. There are three categories of competition: (1) Long Drink (2) After-dinner Cocktail (3) Pre-dinner Cocktail. One category is selected each year. The winner of the Australian title is flown overseas to compete in the competition for the World Titles, which is held every year.

At the 1987 IBA World Championship held in Rome, James Manuel David, the ABG (Long Drink) champion in 1986 for his creation Passionate Scene won the highly-prized World Efficiency Award, and Frank McDermott, ABG champion in 1987, won the World Title in the pre-dinner class with his cocktail Ole.

The ABG has at least one branch in most Australian States. The National Office is in NSW. Alex Beaumont is the National President (phone 02 9262 2119).

The National Presidents of the ABG have been:

1962 - 67	Ian Orton	1992 - 93	Alex Beaumont
1967 - 69	Peter Carlie	1993 - 94	Garry Rand
1969 - 79	Eddie Torado	1994 - 96	Russell Steabben
1979 - 86	Alex Beaumont	1996 -	Alex Beaumont
1986 - 92	Russell Steabben		

19 Winners of the A.B.G. Competition

Australian Champion 1997

Australian Champion 1998

Tiger's Eye

10 mL	Mandarine Napoléon	2	/14
30 mL	Bols Silvertop gin	6	/14
10 mL	Marie Brizard Pear William liqueur	2	/14
15 mL	Pure pear juice	3	/14
5 mL	Lemon juice	1	/14

Ice

METHOD Shake and strain.

GARNISH Lime and mandarin peel.

GLASS Standard cocktail (140 mL).

Created by Barry T. Emerson.

Prince of Darkness

30 mL	Bols brown crème de cacao	6	/17
10 mL	Kahlua	2	/17
5 mL	Bailey's Irish Cream	1	/17
30 mL	Cream	3	/14
10 mL	Monin chocolate mint	1	/14

Crushed ice (frappé style)

METHOD Fill glass with crushed ice. Pour a dash of the brown crème de cacao over the ice. Place remaining ingredients in shaker. Shake and strain into ice-filled glass.

GARNISH Large grated curl of chocolate, sprig of mint, coffee stick.

GLASS Standard cocktail (140 mL).

Created by Ingram Jung.

Glossary

The glossary includes entries on all the products and processes referred to in the text which may need definition. It also includes entries on a wide range of products which the bartender may encounter but which are not referred to in the text. It is therefore a select dictionary of alcoholic liquors as well as a glossary to the text.

Abricotine A French liqueur made from apricots and brandy with a mild almond taste.

Absinthe A strong yellow aniseed and liquorice-flavoured liqueur, banned as toxic in 1915. Pastis is similar, but less strong.

Acqua minerale Italian for mineral water.

Additives Preservatives, colours, flavours, acids, vitamins, or minerals added to beverages.

Advocaat Originally a Dutch product (spelt advokaat), many Australian brands are now available. A blend of egg-yolk, sugar, aromatic spirits and brandy, heated together under constant stirring. The nutritional value of the eggs is fully retained.

Aerated waters Carbonated soft drinks.

Afrikoko A chocolate and coconut liqueur.

Aiguebelle A green liqueur made from 35 different herbs, roots and plants grown in the Provence region of the south of France.

Alcohol The intoxicating ingredient in all fermented and distilled beverages. It is produced by the action of yeast on sugar.

Alcohol by volume The usual measure of alcohol in beverages. See Section 16.

Alcoholic (1) Containing alcohol; intoxicating. (2) Person excessively addicted to alcoholic drinks.

Alcoholometer Device for measuring the level of alcohol in a liquid.

Ale Top-fermented beer. Very little ale, correctly defined, is brewed commercially in Australia, but it is the staple beer in British and Irish pubs. Toohey's Old and Cooper's Sparkling Ale are examples of the rare Australian ales. See also Beer.

Amadeus An Austrian almond and orange-flavoured, cognac-based liqueur.

Amaretto di Saronno An Italian liqueur with an almond and apricot flavour.

Amer Picon A type of bitters. (*Amer* is French for bitters.)

Amontillado A 'medium' style of sherry. See Sherry.

Amourette A violet-coloured French liqueur.

Amsterdam Cherry brandy and advocaat.

Anesone An Italian aniseed and liquorice-flavoured liqueur.

Angelica A sweet yellow Basque liqueur flavoured with angelica.

Angostura Bitters The best-known brand of aromatic bitters used strictly for flavouring (see Bitters). It is widely used in cocktails. Made in Trinidad with gentian and orange peel as its dominant ingredients.

Anisette This French liqueur, sometimes called 'anis', is one of the oldest liqueurs in the world. It is distilled from the finest Alicante aniseed, coriander seed and various other herbs.

Aperitif Drink taken before a meal and designed to sharpen the appetite. Pre-dinner cocktails or dry sherry are examples of drinks usually served as aperitifs.

Aperol Aperitivo A bitter orange-flavored Italian aperitif.

Apple brandy A brandy distilled from apple wine. Calvados is a kind of apple brandy.

Apple cider Fermented apple juice.

Applejack An American apple brandy.

Apricot brandy An apricot-flavoured brandy.

Aqua vitae Brandy and other spirits. (Latin for 'water of life'.)

Aquavit A Scandinavian spirit flavoured with

caraway seed; the same drink is elsewhere called schnapps.

Archers A peach schnapps.

Armagnac A fine brandy produced in the Armagnac region of southern France.

Arrack A clear Asian spirit distilled from various bases and usually aniseed-flavoured. Raki is the Turkish variety.

Asbach Uralt A fine German brandy.

Atholl Brose Traditional Scottish drink made of uncooked oatmeal, honey, cream and malt whisky.

Aurum An Italian triple-sec liqueur, golden in colour.

B.A.C. Blood Alcohol Concentration (for example, .05). See Section 17.

Bacardi Brand name of a famous Caribbean firm of rum producers best known for its light white rums.

Bahia A Brazilian coffee liqueur.

Bailey's Irish Cream A liqueur made with Irish whiskey, blended with chocolate and cream.

Baitz (C.& E.) Melbourne-based company producing a range of liqueurs, etc.

Balthazar Bottle size. Equivalent of sixteen standard bottles (12.8 litres).

Banana liqueur A banana-flavoured liqueur. Popular brands of banana liqueur are produced by Seagram, Suntory, etc. The Suntory version is called Lena banana liqueur.

Bar (1) Counter from which drinks are served. (2) Room where drinks are served, for example lounge bar, public bar.

Barack Palinka A Hungarian apricot brandy.

Bärenfang A German lime and mullein flower liqueur flavoured with honey.

Bar spoon Long-handled stainless steel spoon for serving (see Section 10.6d).

Beer The term used to describe the various liquors brewed from fermented cereals—ales, lager, and stout. The difference between ales and lager is that they are made by different methods of fermentation. The yeasts used are either of a kind which ferment on the top of the liquid (top fermentation) in which case the result is ale, or they sink to the bottom and ferment there (bottom fermentation), in which case the result is lager. Almost all Australian beers are lagers.

See Fermentation, Draught beer, Hops.

Beer with a dash Beer with a dash of lemonade or lime cordial.

Bénédictine DOM One of the most famous French liqueurs. It is golden in colour, highly aromatic and very sweet. It was originally distilled by Benedictine monks. When mixed with an equal amount of brandy the result is called a B and B. DOM stands for the Latin words *Deo Optimo Maximo*, which mean 'To God, the most good, the most great'.

Beverage Any liquid intended for drinking.

Bitter Beer with a bitter taste from an unusually high proportion of hops.

Bitters Essences made from roots, fruit, and peel compounded with alcohol. Sometimes bitters are taken for digestive or medicinal purposes. Some brands of bitters, for example Campari, are served as drinks mixed usually with soda. Others, most notably Angostura Bitters, are concentrated essences used only for flavouring.

Black and Tan Half a light-coloured draught beer (traditionally a bitter) and half stout.

Blackberry Nip A fortified wine with a blackberry flavour.

Black Tie A coffee liqueur.

Blend Cocktail mixing term. Blended ingredients are mixed in a blender. See Section 7 on Mixing Drinks and Mixing Terms.

Blood Alcohol Concentration (B.A.C.) See Section 17.

Blue curaçao See Curaçao.

Boilermaker Whisky with a beer chaser.

Bols Famous Dutch company which makes a variety of advocaats, maraschinos, liqueurs, etc.

Bond The store in which alcoholic beverages are kept under customs and excise supervision before duty has been paid. To pay duty on and take delivery of alcoholic beverages in bond is to 'clear from bond'.

Boonekamp A Dutch aromatic bitters.

Bouquet The fragrant impression left after 'nosing' a beverage.

Bourbon One of several kinds of American whiskey, originally produced in Bourbon County, Kentucky. U.S. regulations require bourbon whiskey to be made from not less than 51 per cent corn grain and aged for at least two years in new charred oak barrels. The charring of the barrels gives bourbon its distinctive character.

Brandy A spirit distilled from any fruit but most commonly from grapes. If fruits other than grapes are used then they are included in the name, e.g. cherry brandy. The word 'brandy' used alone in the name implies grape brandy. Cognac and armagnac are high quality styles of brandy, usually served neat. See Cognac.

Breathalyser Device for measuring alcohol on the breath.

Breathe Be exposed to fresh air as when a bottle of wine is opened to allow it to 'breathe' some time before it is served.

Breath test Measure of alcohol on the breath by means of a breathalyser.

Bristol Cream A brand of cream sherry.

Brontë An English honey and brandy liqueur.

Brut A French term indicating the driest of champagnes. Pronounced broot.

Build Cocktail mixing term. To build a drink is to mix it in the glass. See Section 7 on Mixing Terms.

Bundaberg rum A dark rum. The largest-selling rum in Australia.

Burgundy Burgundy is the English name for the French province of Bourgogne, famous for its wines, both red and white. The word 'burgundy' has been used in Australia as a generic description of a style of red wine—soft and round without the astringent finish of 'claret' because there is less tannin—but the term is no longer used on Australian red wine labels. However, the use of the term 'white burgundy' still survives in some well-established Australian brand names, for example Houghton's White Burgundy.

Byrrh A bitter wine-based aperitif flavoured with quinine.

Cadbury Cream Liqueur A liqueur made with French brandy, blended with Cadbury chocolate and cream.

Calisay A Spanish sweet herb liqueur.

Calvados An apple brandy made from cider in the Calvados region of northern France.

Campari A brand of Italian bitters; a bitter-sweet aperitif.

Canadian Club A brand of Canadian whisky.

Cane spirit Pure clear spirit distilled from fermented cane sugar, useful in cocktail mixes. Mainstay is a popular brand of cane spirit.

Carafe Glass container used for serving house wine or water.

Carambola Star fruit.

Carbonate Make effervescent by injecting carbon dioxide (CO_2).

Carbonated wines Sparkling wines made by injecting still wine with carbon dioxide (CO_2).

Cask (1) Plastic or foil-lined cardboard box. (2) Barrel, especially one containing alcohol.

Cassis Blackcurrant liqueur. See Crème de cassis.

Cava See Kava.

Cellar Place for storing wines or for storing and tapping kegs of beer.

Cerasella An Italian cherry liqueur.

Chambord A black raspberry liqueur from Burgundy in France.

Champagne The most famous kind of French sparkling wine. See also Méthode champenoise.

Chartreuse A famous French liqueur which contains over 130 herbs and spices. Green and yellow styles are made, the yellow being less alcoholic and sweeter. The liqueur is still made by Carthusian monks.

Chaser A measure of spirits bought together with a longer drink and consumed (often skulled) after it, e.g. 'beer with a whisky chaser'.

Chéri-Suisse A Swiss cherry and chocolate liqueur.

Cherry advocaat A pre-mixed combination of advocaat and cherry brandy.

Cherry brandy A fruit liqueur made of the juice of ripe dark cherries and the distillate of fermented cherry juice. The pleasant taste of almonds in cherry brandy is obtained from the aroma of crushed dry cherry stones. Peter Heering is a brand of cherry brandy.

Cherry Heering Former name of a brand of cherry brandy. See Peter Heering.

Chianti An Italian dry red wine.

Cider A fermented drink made from apples. Both alcoholic and non-alcoholic varieties are available

Cinzano A brand of vermouth, available in sweet, dry and bianco styles. See Vermouth.

Claret Red wine either from the Bordeaux region of France or of similar type. Clarets are medium-bodied and have a distinctively astringent after-taste because of their high tannin content.

Clayton's Clayton's Cola Tonic, usually referred to simply as 'Clayton's', is a non-alcoholic cola tonic used in many non-alcoholic drinks.

Cleopatra A chocolate and orange liqueur.

CO_2 Carbon dioxide. Gas used to carbonate beverages.

Cobbler A long cooling drink made with either spirits or wine, with fruit juice or soda and plenty of ice.

Coconut cream A non-alcoholic concentrate of coconut pulp, sugar syrup, etc. used, for example, in Pina Colada.

Coconut rum A white rum flavoured with essences from coconuts. Brand names include Malibu and CocoRibe.

CocoRibe A brand of coconut rum.

Cognac The most famous brandy in the world. Cognac can only be produced legally in the area surrounding the town of Cognac in south-western France. The letters VSOP on a bottle of cognac stand for Very Superior Old Pale. Sometimes the letters F and X are also used. F stands for Fine and X for Extra. Champagne cognac has nothing to do with champagne the sparkling wine. The best part of the Cognac district happens also to be called Champagne, and champagne cognac is cognac of superior quality.

Cointreau A French liqueur, one of the best-known triple sec curaçaos. It is colourless and orange-flavoured. The orange flavour is derived from the peel of small bitter curaçao oranges mixed with a small amount of valencia orange peel. When Cointreau is served on the rocks it turns milky white.

Cola A carbonated drink flavoured with the seed of the west African cola tree.

Collins A long drink made with a spirit, sugar and soda.

Continental Distillers A Sydney-based company producing a range of liqueurs, etc.

Coolers See Wine Cooler.

Cordial A flavoured and sweetened drink made from fruit. In the USA another word for a liqueur.

Cordial Médoc A French liqueur made from cognac, claret, herbs, orange curaçao and crème de cacao.

Corkage A fee charged by a licensed estab-lishment for serving alcohol that the customer has not bought on the premises.

Corked wine Wine permanently spoiled by a mouldy cork.

Coruba rum A dark rum made in Jamaica.

Cream liqueurs A relatively recent development made possible by technical advances. Cream, spirit and flavourings are mixed to make rich thick liqueurs. Bailey' s Irish Cream is the best-known example.

Crema de Lima A Spanish lime-flavoured liqueur.

Crème The name used for many heavily-sug-ared usually not very alcoholic liqueurs each with one distinct flavour, e.g. crème de menthe (peppermint-flavoured) or crème de cacao (chocolate-flavoured).

Crème d'amandes An almond-flavoured liqueur.

Crème d'ananas A pineapple liqueur.

Crème de banane A sweet liqueur made from a maceration of bananas and alcohol.

Crème de cacao A liqueur made from cocoa beans and vanilla. It comes in two colours: brown and white.

Crème de café A coffee liqueur.

Crème de cassis A liqueur made from black currants. It is regarded as a health-giving digestive.

Crème de ciel An orange-flavoured liqueur.

Crème de cumin A caraway seed-flavoured liqueur.

Crème de fraises A liqueur flavoured with strawberries.

Crème de fraises des bois A wild strawberry-flavoured liqueur.

Crème de framboise A raspberry-coloured and flavoured liqueur.

Crème de Grand Marnier A liqueur made with Grand Marnier blended with cream.

Crème de guignolet A cherry-flavoured liqueur.

Crème de Kobai A Japanese plum-flavoured liqueur.

Crème de menthe An aromatic liqueur with considerable digestive properties and a fresh cool taste. It is distilled over soft peppermint beans. It is available in either green or white styles, but the green style is the most popular.

Crème de Mocca A liqueur made from roasted coffee beans and with added raw cane sugar.

Crème de noix A walnut-flavoured liqueur.

Crème de noyau A liqueur flavoured with peach kernels.

Crème de noyeau An almond-flavoured liqueur, pink or white in colour.

Crème de poire A pear-flavoured liqueur.

Crème de prune A plum-flavoured liqueur.

Crème de prunelle A plum-flavoured liqueur.

Crème de roses A pink rose-flavoured liqueur.

Crème de thé A tea-flavoured liqueur.

Crème de vanille A vanilla-flavoured liqueur.

Crème de violette A violet-flavoured liqueur.

Crème Yvette An American liqueur made from petals of the Parma violet. It is named in honour of the French actress Yvette Guilbert.

Crusta A cocktail with a sugar frosting.

Cuarenta-y-Tres Another name for the Spanish herb liqueur Licor 43.

Cup A mixed drink, normally wine-based, made for a number of people, similar to a punch, except that a cup is usually cold. See also Pimm's.

Curaçao Curaçaos date back to the seventeenth century when Dutch traders brought back oranges from the Curaçao islands in the West Indies. It is made from a mixture of peel from curaçao and valencia oranges. The most common colour is white, but other colours are available: orange, red, green and blue.

Danzka A popular brand of vodka. It comes in a variety of flavours.

Dark rum A dark-coloured rum aged in oak barrels and coloured with caramel. See also Rum, Bacardi, Demerara rum and Jamaica rum.

Dash An inexact mixing term — about 5 mL.

Decant To pour a liquid, usually wine, out of the bottle into a glass container to separate the pure liquid from any sediment and, in the case of wine, to let it breathe.

Demerara A light brown raw cane sugar.

Demerara rum Dark rum of a style originally made in Guyana.

Demitasse A small cup, used typically for an espresso or 'short black' coffee.

Digestif Drink taken after a meal to help digestion, especially a liqueur.

Distillation The process of making spirits by heating fermented liquids to vapour and then, by cooling the vapour to condense it, achieving a purified spirit. See also Fermentation.

DOM See Bénédictine.

Dram Scottish term for a measure of spirits, usually Scotch whisky.

Drambuie The oldest and most famous brand of liqueur with a Scotch whisky base. It is flavoured with herbs and heather honey. The name is an Anglicized version of Gaelic words which mean 'the drink that satisfies'.

Draught (draft) beer Beer drawn from a keg, called 'bulk beer' in the industry, as opposed to 'packaged beer' (sold in bottles or cans).

Drops on the Rocks A blend of herbs and spices and limes.

Dr Pepper Beer with a dash of amaretto.

Dry Dry ginger ale.

Dubonnet A brand of dark red aperitif with a slight quinine flavour.

Dutch gin Gin produced in Holland. See Genever gin.

Eau-de-vie French for 'water of life'. A spirit produced from fermented and distilled grape or other fruit juice.

Egg-nog A punch consisting of hot or cold spirits, wine, cider, or beer with eggs and milk mixed in. Holiday Egg-nog is an example. (See Holiday Egg-nog in recipes.)

Fermentation The process by which a liquid with sugar in it is converted into alcohol by the action of yeast. The process occurs naturally. It is the basis of all beers and wines and is the first stage in the making of spirits. See also Beer.

Fernet Branca A brand of Italian bitters made of roots and herbs.

Fino Pale dry sherry. See Sherry.

Fior d'Alpi / Fior d'Alpe Flower of the Alps. A very sweet Italian liqueur made from a mixture of herbs. The bottles have a sprig of a herb in them round which sugar crystallises.

Fizz (1) A long drink cocktail made with soda, a spirit and sugar syrup. (2) Jocular name for sparkling wine, e.g. champagne.

Flagon Large wine bottle (2 litres) popular for table wines before the development of

the cask and still used for cheaper fortified wines, e.g. sherry.

Flip Drink containing eggs and cream, e.g.
rum flip, beer flip.

Float (1) Mixing term. See Section 7. (2)
Change placed in the till before trading
begins.

Florenza A hazel-nut liqueur similar to
Frangelico.

Forbidden Fruit An American grapefruit
and honey liqueur.

Fortified wine Wine that has been strength-
ened by the addition of grape spirit. The
spirit acts as a preservative as well as
strengthening the wine. Port and sherry
are examples of fortified wines.

Fraisia A French strawberry-flavoured
liqueur.

Frangelico A hazel-nut liqueur.

Frappé Any liqueur which is served over
crushed ice. *Frappé* is French for beaten
or crushed.

French Term used to describe dry vermouth,
i.e. French-style vermouth. Used, for
example, in a Gin-and-French.

Frigola A thyme-flavoured liqueur from the
Spanish Mediterranean island of Ibiza.

Frosting The effect achieved when sugar
adheres to glass. To frost a glass, wet the
rim of the glass with a slice of lemon and
then dip the glass in sugar. See Section 4
on Garnishes.

Galliano A golden yellow herb liqueur which
comes from Milan in Italy. It is named
after a Major Galliano who distinguished
himself during the Italian-Abyssinian war
of 1896. See also Galliano varieties
(below).

Galliano varieties:
Black Galliano (black sambuca) is elder-
berry-flavoured.
Blue Galliano is orange-flavoured.
Brown Galliano (amaretto) is almond-
flavoured.
Green Galliano is mint-flavoured.
Red Galliano is cherry-flavoured.
White Galliano (sambuca) is elderberry-
flavoured.

Garnish A decoration for a drink which may
be edible, inedible, or a combination of
both (for example, a pineapple wedge
with a parasol attached). See Section 4.

Generic Of a particular kind or from a particular area, e.g. burgundy, claret,

sparkling wine, crème de menthe, cherry
brandy—as opposed to varietal or proprietary.

Genever gin Dutch gin, sometimes called
Hollands, distilled fermented rye, barley
and maize. It is flavoured with juniper
berries. Genever is a corruption of
genièvre, the French for juniper. See Gin.

Gentian (bitter) A liquor extracted from the
root of the gentian plant.

Gin The base material for the production of
gin is highly rectified grain alcohol which
is distilled over selected natural herbs.
These include juniper berries, angelica
roots, coriander seed, cassia bark, orange,
and orris root. There are two principal
varieties of gin: London Dry and
Genever. London Dry gin is usually used
in cocktails. Genever or Hollands gin,
which comes from the Netherlands, has a
distinctive flavour which makes it less
suitable for mixing. It is usually served
neat. See Genever gin.

Ginger ale An aerated non-alcoholic ginger-
flavoured drink often called dry ginger
ale, or just 'dry'.

Ginger beer A slightly alcoholic drink (below
2% alc/vol) made of ginger, sugar, water
and yeast.

Ginger wine See Green Ginger Wine.

Gin liqueur Gin-flavoured liqueur.

Glayva A Scottish liqueur similar to
Drambuie.

Glen Mist A Scotch whisky-based liqueur
flavoured with herbs, honey and spices.

Glögg A Swedish hot punch similar to glühwein.

Glühwein A kind of mulled wine. See
recipes.

Goldkenn A Swiss chocolate liqueur.

Goldwasser A crystal-clear German liqueur.
It is distilled from a large number of
herbs, seeds, and roots bound together by
its main component, curaçao orange peel.
It is given a special charm by the small
fragments of genuine gold leaf floating in
it. It is not particularly suitable for use in
cocktails and long drinks and it is therefore usually served neat.

Gomme syrup See Sugar syrup.

Grand Marnier A French liqueur made with
cognac and oranges. There are two varieties—red ribbon and yellow ribbon—the
red being the more alcoholic and the bet-
ter-known.

Grappa An Italian spirit distilled from the remnants of grapes (skins, stalks, and pulp) after the juice has been crushed out and drawn off.

Green beer Unmatured young beer.

Green Ginger Wine A wine made from fruit and flavoured with ginger.

Grenadine A red cordial flavoured with pomegranate. It is primarily used as a sweetening and colouring agent in drinks.

Grog Originally a mixture of rum and water issued to sailors in the Royal Navy. Today grog is slang for alcohol.

Guignolet A French cherry-flavoured liqueur.

Guinness The most famous brand of stout. See Stout.

Happy hour An allotted time of the day usually at the end of office hours when the drinks are cheaper.

Hard liquor Liquor over 37% alc/vol, usually spirits.

Heather Cream A Scottish malt whisky and cream liqueur.

Highball A measure of spirit with ice and ginger ale or soda served in a Highball glass.

Hock German, or German-style, dry white wine.

Hollands Dutch gin. See Gin and Genever gin.

Hops The cones or fruit clusters of a climbing plant used to give bitterness to beer.

House wine Low-priced wine bought in bulk by an establishment, sometimes served in a carafe.

Indian tonic Tonic water; a non-alcoholic carbonated drink flavoured with quinine; it is often mixed with gin as a gin-and-tonic.

Infusion Technique of extracting flavour by soaking a flavouring agent in warm spirit used in liqueur production.

Intoxicate To make drunk. See Section 17 on the Responsible Service of Alcohol.

Irish Mist A honey-flavoured Irish liqueur similar to Drambuie.

Irish whiskey Irish whiskey is made from fermented barley by a different process from that used to make Scotch malt and grain whiskies. It is distilled in pot stills. It has a distinctive clear light flavour. See Whisky.

Italian Term used to describe sweet (Italian-style) vermouth, as in a gin-and-Italian (Gin-and-It). See recipes.

Izarra A French liqueur made from armagnac, eau-de-vie, fruits, honey and flowers.

Jack Daniel's A famous brand of Tennessee whiskey.

Jamaica rum Traditional Jamaica rum is full-bodied and dark brown with a pungent aroma and assertive flavour. It is aged in oak for at least five years.

Jenever Dutch gin (an alternative spelling of Genever).

Jeroboam Bottle size. Four bottles (3.2 litres).

Jigger An American bar measure—43 mL (1.5 ounces).

Julep A long drink cocktail, mint-flavoured and served with crushed ice, popular in the southern States of the USA.

Kahlua A brandy-based liqueur flavoured with coffee.

Kava An intoxicating South Pacific drink prepared from the root of the kava plant, a kind of pepper plant.

Keuck A Turkish coffee liqueur.

Kirsch A clear cherry brandy. *Kirsche* is the German for cherry.

Kirschwasser A German cherry brandy.

Korn A German clear grain spirit, an abbreviation for Kornbranntwein.

Krupnik A Polish vodka-based liqueur flavoured with honey and herbs.

Kümmel A Dutch liqueur flavoured with caraway, cumin, fennel and orris root. Normally served over ice.

L Litre. The basic unit of capacity. See mL.

Lager Bottom-fermented beer. Almost all Australian beers are lagers. See Beer.

Lay-back Alcohol poured into or mixed in the mouth of a drinker while the drinker lies back onto the bar or in a chair.

Lemon brandy Lemon-flavoured brandy.

Lemon Ruski A pre-mixed alcoholic drink containing vodka, wine, soda water and lemon juice. 5% alc/vol.

Lena Banana Liqueur A brand of banana liqueur made by Suntory. *Lena* means yellow in Tahitian.

Le Touche A liqueur made from armagnac, oranges and herbs.

Licensed With a licence to serve alcoholic

beverages, so 'licensed hotel', 'licensed restaurant', etc.

Licor 43 A Spanish liqueur made from 43 herbs, also called Cuarenta-y-Tres.

Light beer Low alcohol beer (approx. 3% alc/vol).

Light rum Clear or pale-coloured rum with a light molasses flavour. See Rum.

Light wine Low alcohol wine.

Lillet A French brand of vermouth, consisting of wine fortified with armagnac, herbs and fruit.

Liqueur Any sweetened and flavoured alcoholic drink, but the term is usually used to indicate a drink of this kind most commonly taken after a meal (often also used as an ingredient in cocktails). Many liqueurs have digestive qualities and many of them were originally devised for medicinal purposes. In the USA liqueurs are known as cordials. The term liqueur is sometimes also used in connection with old brandies, ports and muscats.

Liquor Any alcoholic drink, especially distilled spirits such as whisky and brandy.

Lochan Ora A Scottish liqueur based, like Drambuie, on honey and whisky.

London dry A style of gin. See Gin.

Long drink (cocktail) A cocktail served in a Highball glass; a judging category for cocktail competitions. See Section 1.

Maceration A process of crushing and soaking and so implanting a flavour, for example in a liqueur.

Madeira A fortified wine with a distinctive 'burnt' taste. There are styles ranging from dry to very sweet. The original madeiras come from the Portuguese island of Madeira.

Magnum Bottle size: equivalent of two standard bottles (1.6 litres).

Mainstay A brand of cane spirit from Mauritius.

Maker's Mark A Kentucky straight whiskey (bourbon). S 1V is the mark of the maker on each bottle. The mark is that of Bill Samuels, Senior.

Malibu A brand of rum-based coconut liqueur.

Malt whisky Scotch whisky made exclusively from fermented malt barley. Most Scotch whiskies are a blend of malt and grain whisky.

Mandarine Napoléon A Belgian liqueur distilled from tangerine peel and compounded with cognac. There are other less expensive 'mandarin' liqueurs.

Mango liqueur A mango-flavoured liqueur. A popular brand is made by Suntory.

Maraschino An Italian liqueur produced from the distillation of sour cherries including the crushed kernels.

Maraschino cherries Cherries preserved in a non-alcoholic maraschino juice.

Marie Brizard French company making a range of generic liqueurs.

Marsala A sweet fortified wine. When flavoured with egg yolk it is called marsala all'uovo.

Martini A gin-based cocktail, and also the brand name of a range of vermouths.

Masticha A Greek brandy-based liqueur.

Metaxa A Greek company producing superior brandy and ouzo.

Méthode champenoise Sparkling wine made by the traditional method used in the Champagne region of France. It has a special sparkle produced by second fermentation in the bottle.

Methuselah Bottle size. Equivalent of eight standard bottles (6.4 litres).

Mezcal A Mexican spirit distilled from the mezcal azul variety of cactus. Tequila is a high-quality kind of mezcal.

Mickey Finn A very strong drink, often drugged, used to intoxicate or stupefy an unsuspecting drinker. (Slang.)

Midori Citrus A pre-mixed mildly alcoholic drink containing Midori Melon Liqueur with natural orange, grapefruit and lime flavours.

Midori Melon Liqueur A green Japanese liqueur made from honeydew melon often called simply 'Midori'. *Midori* means green in Japanese.

Mirabelle A French plum brandy made from scented yellow (cherry) plums

Mise-en-place The assembling of all necessary equipment and ingredients in their proper places before beginning work. See Section 9.

mL Millilitre. Unit of capacity. One thousandth part of a litre.

Mocktail A non-alcoholic cocktail.

Monin A French company making liqueurs (such as Monin Triple Lime Liqueur) and also a huge range of concentrated fruit-flavoured non-alcoholic syrups, commonly used in cocktail-making as a substitute for expensive liqueurs.

Mount Gay rum A Jamaican-style rum made in Barbados.

Moselle A white wine made in the Mösel (French Moselle) river district of Germany, or (loosely) a similar type of moderately sweet wine made elsewhere.

Muddle Mixing term. To stir and mash.

Mull To warm a drink; a warm drink.

Mulled wine Wine warmed and mixed with sugar, spices, etc. Glühwein is a kind of mulled wine.

Muscat A fortified sweet dessert wine with a characteristic aroma and very rich flavour made from muscat grapes. Rutherglen in northern Victoria is particularly famous for its muscats.

Muselet The muzzle or wire clip which helps to hold in the cork on a bottle of champagne or other sparkling wine.

Nip A standard measure (30 mL).

Nose The smell of a wine, a combination of its aroma and its bouquet. To 'nose' a wine is to sniff it to assess its bouquet.

Oke Short for okolehao.

Okolehao A Hawaiian spirit distilled from roots of the ti plant, also called oke.

Old Krupnik A Polish honey and herb vodka-based liqueur.

Oloroso Gold nutty sherry style. See Sherry.

On-the-rocks Mixing term. A drink served 'on-the-rocks' is served over a large quantity of cubed ice.

Opal Nera Black Sambuca.

Orange bitters A kind of concentrated bitters used for flavouring, similar to Angostura Bitters.

Orange curaçao See Curaçao.

Orgeat syrup A non-alcoholic syrup flavoured with almonds.

Original Peachtree Liqueur See Peachtree Liqueur.

Ouzo (or oyzo) A grape spirit flavoured with aniseed, originally from Greece.

Overproof Term used to describe spirits (usually rum) which are stronger than proof (more than 100° proof). See Section 16 on Alcoholic Strengths.

Oyzo See Ouzo.

Palate The term used to describe the taste of wine.

Parfait Amour (Perfect Love) A soft lilac-coloured liqueur made from curaçao, orange peel, vanilla pods, almonds and roses.

Par stock Minimum bar (or cellar) stock level.

Pasha A Turkish coffee liqueur.

Pastis A French spirit flavoured with aniseed and liquorice. Ricard and Pernod are brands of pastis.

Peach liqueur Peach-flavoured liqueur.

Peachtree Liqueur A clear peach-flavoured liqueur made by the Dutch company De Kuyper.

Pear brandy Pear-flavoured liqueur.

Pernod Brand name of a French aperitif with an aniseed flavour, a kind of pastis.

Perrier Brand name of the most famous kind of French mineral water.

Peter Heering A Danish firm which makes a famous cherry brandy formerly known as Cherry Heering (now Peter Heering's Cherry Liqueur) and other liqueurs.

Pick-me-up A hangover cure. See pick-me-ups in the index.

Pilsner A much-imitated kind of lager originally made in the town of Pilsen (Plzen) in the Czech Republic.

Pimm's No 1 Cup The original and best-known of the 'cups' marketed by Pimm's. It has a gin base. A Pimm's is usually served as a long drink with a combination of lemonade and dry ginger ale, ice and fruit. See recipes.

Pisang Ambon A banana and herb liqueur.

Pisco A South American brandy.

Poire Williams A spirit distilled from an infusion of williams pears.

Port A fortified sweet wine originally from Portugal. Various styles are made: vintage, ruby and tawny. Most ports are red, but white port is made.

Portagaf Stout and lemonade.

Post-mix A device for mixing and serving carbonated beverages. Water is carbonated with CO_2 gas and automatically mixed with a syrup of the desired flavour, e.g. lemonade or ginger ale, at the point of sale.

Poteen (potcheen) Home or illegally-made Irish whiskey.

Pot still The traditional kind of still used to

distil fine brandies and some kinds of whiskies. The liquor has to be distilled in batches. Most commercial spirits are distilled on continuous stills, sometimes called Coffey stills after their inventor.

Pousse café Another name for a layered cocktail.

Pre-mixed alcoholic drink (cocktail) A popular form of packaging. Most spirit and liqueur companies package their products in pre-mixed bottles and cans. Some examples include Midori and lemonade, Jim Beam and cola and the U.D.L. (United Distillers) range. New products emerge all the time. Some more recent arrivals include Two Dogs, Sub-Zero, Lemon Ruski and XLR8.

Proof A standard of strength of distilled alcoholic liquors. US proof is 50% alc/vol. See Section 16 on Alcoholic Strengths.

Proprietary Property of a specific owner; product of a single company. Compare generic.

Punch A drink usually of wine or spirits mixed with fruit juices, cream, sugar, spices, fruit, etc.

Punsch A Swedish mixed drink consisting of a brandy base blended with arrack and wine.

Punt e Mes An Italian bitter-sweet aperitif flavoured with quinine.

Q.F. A cocktail: polite abbreviation for Quick Fuck. See recipes.

Quetsch. A clear brandy made from black plums.

Quinine A bitter ingredient in many vermouths, liqueurs and tonic waters.

Raki A Turkish aniseed liqueur, a variety of arrack.

Rectify Purify by repeated distillation.

Rehoboam Bottle size. Equivalent of six standard bottles (4.8 litres).

Reishu A Japanese melon liqueur.

Retsina A traditional Greek wine flavoured with pine resin which acts as a preservative.

Rhine Riesling See Riesling.

Rhum Negrita A fine Caribbean rum from Martinique.

Ricard A brand of pastis.

Rickey A long drink cocktail with lime, an alcohol and soda, similar to a Collins but

without the sugar.

Riesling Grape variety, formerly also called Rhine Riesling. The word 'riesling' has also been used to indicate a generic style of dry white wine, not necessarily made from Riesling grapes.

Rosso Antico An Italian aperitif infused with aromatic herbs.

Royal Chocolate Liqueur A chocolate mint liqueur.

R.S.A. Responsible Service of Alcohol. See Section 17.

R.T.D. Short for Ready to Drink. See Pre-mixed alcoholic drink.

Rum A spirit made from sugar cane. There are many styles of rum with very different characteristics. See also Dark rum, Light rum, Jamaica rum and Bacardi.

Rye American or Canadian whisky made from rye and other grains.

Sabra An Israeli liqueur flavoured with orange and chocolate.

Sake Traditional Japanese rice liquor usually served warm. It has a delicate sweet flavour but a dry finish. It is served in a small porcelain pot with tiny cups.

Salmanazar Bottle size. Equivalent of twelve standard bottles (9.6 litres).

Sambuca A strong Italian liqueur made from an infusion of liquorice and witch elder bush.

Sauternes A famous French sweet white dessert wine.

Schnapps White spirit from northern Europe. Schnapps is available in a variety of flavours. The name means gasp or snatch, which is often the result when you drink schnapps ice cold in one gulp.

Scotch Any whisky produced in Scotland. See Whisky.

Scrumpy A rough, strong cider.

Scull To drink in a single gulp, or without taking a breath.

Seagram A very large Canadian company with interests throughout the world. Produces a variety of whiskies, liqueurs, etc.

Sec Literally French for 'dry' but confusingly often applied to drinks which are nearer to sweet than dry. See Triple Sec.

Sekt The best quality of German or German-style sparkling wine.

Shandy Beer and lemonade.

Sheridans A liqueur made with Irish whiskey blended with chocolate, coffee, cream and vanilla. The bottle has a split chamber.

Sherry A fortified wine originally from Jerez in Spain. There are several styles: Fino: very pale, light and dry, with a delicate aroma. Amontillado: amber-coloured medium dry with a nutty flavour. Oloroso: gold-coloured and heavy bodied with a nutty flavour. Olorosos vary from dry to sweet. Cream: light bodied and very sweet.

Shochu A Japanese schnapps-type spirit.

Shooter A layered cocktail of spirits and/or liqueurs with no mixer, or a neat spirit or liqueur, served in a shot glass or a test-tube and usually skulled.

Shot A single measure of alcohol (usually spirit), a nip.

Skull To down a drink in a single gulp.

Slammer A drink consumed in one gulp after which the glass is slammed on the bar. See Tequila Slammer in recipes.

Sling A long drink cocktail with a gin base. Singapore Sling is the most famous example (see recipe).

Slivovitz A Balkan plum brandy.

Sloe gin Gin flavoured with sloe berries.

Smash A short julep.

Snifter Another name for a brandy balloon.

Soda In Australia, UK and New Zealand short for soda water, but in USA the word can mean any effervescent soft drink.

Soda water Water made effervescent by injection with CO_2.

Sours Spirit sours are made up of a spirit, fresh lemon or lime juice and sugar or sugar syrup. Egg white is frequently used and this will change the taste and appearance of the drink. Sours are traditionally mixed in a cocktail shaker, but today they are sometimes prepared using a blender. Care should be taken with the quantities of ice and egg white as the blender is far more efficient than the shaker. See recipe for Whiskey Sour.

Southern Comfort An American liquor distilled from grain, similar to bourbon but with a peach flavour. There is some dispute as to whether it is a liqueur or a spirit.

Sparkling wine Wines with a sparkling fizz in them caused by naturally fermented carbon dioxide. If CO_2 has been injected under pressure rather than caused by natural fermentation, the resulting wine should be called 'carbonated wine' not sparkling wine. Champagne is the most famous kind of sparkling wine.

Spirits The general term for all distilled spirits.

Split A term used to describe small bottles (about 285 mL), typically of effervescent drinks like soda or tonic. Their contents are more likely to have retained all their sparkle than those of larger bottles which are often not all used at once.

Standard drink See Section 17 on the Responsible Service of Alcohol.

Still Apparatus used for distilling spirits. See Pot still.

Stinger Alcoholic soda water with separate flavoured test tubes for mixing.

Stoli Short for Stolichnaya vodka.

Stolichnaya A popular brand of Russian vodka made from 100 per cent grain spirits.

Stout A very dark beer, made with roasted barley. Guinness is the best-known brand of stout.

Straight up Mixing term. Served with no ice. neat.

Strawberry liqueur A strawberry-flavoured liqueur. Popular brands of strawberry liqueur are produced by Seagram, Suntory, etc.

Strega (the witch) A yellow liqueur produced in Italy, similar to Galliano.

Sub-Zero A pre-mixed alcoholic drink containing alcoholic soda. Sub-Zero is available in several flavours.

Sugar syrup A sugar or 'simple' syrup, often called gomme syrup. It is a combination of sugar and very hot water used for sweetening beverages. See Section 6 for instructions on how to make it.

Suntory Japanese company making beer, liqueurs, whisky, etc.

Swizzle Another name for a long drink, especially one made in quantity in a jug with soda, sweetened with sugar, and served in a Highball glass.

Syrups Sweet non-alcoholic fruit essences used in many mixed drinks. Grenadine and cassis are examples of fruit syrups. See also Monin (syrups).

Tabasco A pungent pepper made from the fruit of capsicum; a sauce made from this pepper.

Table wines Still wines which are not fortified or flavoured, customarily served with meals at table. Table wines normally range from 9-14% alc/vol.

Tannin Acidic astringent substance present in all wines, but particularly red wines. It greatly affects the palate of wine.

Tennessee whiskey A kind of whiskey made in Tennessee (USA) with a distinctive soft, sweet flavour.

Tequila A Mexican spirit distilled from the cactus-like mezcal azul plant. See also Mezcal.

Tia Maria A rum-based coffee-flavoured liqueur from Jamaica.

Tiquira A high strength spirit from Brazil made from tapioca root.

Toddy A mixture of hot water and spirit, usually whisky, sometimes with lemon and sugar.

Tokay In Australia a sweet pale fortified dessert wine similar to muscat. The original Hungarian Tokay is an unfortified very sweet dessert wine similar to Sauternes.

Tonic See Indian Tonic.

T. Q. HOT A popular Mexican tequila-based liqueur.

Triple Sec A kind of sweet, white curaçao. See also Cointreau.

Two Dogs A pre-mixed alcoholic drink consisting of a lemon-flavoured brew.

Underberg A brand of German bitters. See Bitters.

Van der Hum A curaçao-style South African liqueur flavoured with *naartjies* (mandarins). Van der Hum means (more or less) 'Mr What's-his-name' in Afrikaans.

Van der Mint A Dutch chocolate and mint liqueur.

Varietal Made from a particular variety (of grape), e.g. Shiraz or Chardonnay, as opposed to generic.

Vermouth A flavoured fortified wine available in many varieties. There are three principal styles: dry (or French) which is dry and 'white'; sweet (or Italian) which is sweet and red; and bianco which is golden-coloured and medium sweet. The word vermouth comes from the German *Wermut*, meaning wormwood, which is one of the many herbs used to flavour vermouth.

Virgin A cocktail with the main alcoholic ingredients left out. For example a Bloody Mary with no vodka is called a Virgin Mary.

Vodka A spirit distilled from a base of grain, and highly rectified. Modern vodka is normally filtered through charcoal to ensure absolute purity, which makes it an excellent mixer in cocktails. However there are flavoured vodkas, e.g. the Polish vodka Zubrowka, which has a delicate aromatic bouquet and contains a stem of zubrowka grass in the bottle.

VSOP Very Superior Old Pale. See Cognac.

Waiter's friend A combination of bottle-opener and corkscrew. See the illustration in Section 10.4.

Wee dram Scottish for small amount of alcohol, usually neat whisky.

Wheel Garnishing term to describe a slice cut across the grain of a piece of fruit. See Garnishes (Section 4.6).

Whisky All whiskies are distilled from corn (barley, rye, wheat, or maize, or a combination of them). The main types are Scotch (blended or malt), Irish, Canadian, American (bourbon, rye and Tennessee), and Japanese. American and Irish whiskies are spelt 'whiskey', while Scotch, Canadian, and Japanese use the spelling 'whisky'.

Wine cooler A mixture of fruit juice and wine of varying alcoholic content, usually packaged in casks and served neat in a wine glass.

Wisniowska A Polish cherry vodka: it is not as sweet as cherry brandy.

Worcestershire sauce A sauce made of vinegar, molasses, sugar, spices, etc. used in some cocktails.

X L R 8 A pre-mixed alcoholic drink, containing alcoholic cola.

Zubrowka A kind of Polish vodka. See Vodka.

Index

References to cocktail recipes appear in alphabetical order in the index in **bold type**. Cocktails are also gathered together in groups of cocktails of a single category, e.g. COLADAS. Such group names are printed in BOLD CAPITALS. References to illustrations are in brackets. See also the Glossary for particular liquors and technical terms.

A.B.G., see Australian Bartenders Guild.
after-dinner cocktails 9, 167
After Dinner Mint (shooter) 12
Aida's Curse 12
alcohol 160-2, 163-4, 166, 169
    responsible service of, 163-6
alcoholic strengths 160-2, 166
Alexander, see Brandy Alexander and also
    Cherry Alexander and Midori Alexander.
Amaretto Sour, see Whiskey Sour (note).
Americano 12
Anobolic Steroids (shooter) 12
Angel's Tip (shooter) 12
Angry Fijian (shooter) 14
Apotheke (pick-me-up) 14
Apple Breaker (mocktail) 14
Apple Delight (mocktail) 14
Apple Jack 14
Arcadia 14
ashtrays 157
Australia III (13), 15, (123)
Australia IV (mocktail) 15
Australian Bartenders Guild 11, 167-8
Australian Crawl 15

B and B 15
B 52, No 1 (short or shooter) 15
B 52, No 2 (long) 16
Bacardi Cocktail 16
balloon glass 152
Banana Bender 16
Banana Colada 16
Banana Daiquiri 16
Banana Fizz 16
Banana Margarita 17
Banana Mender (mocktail) 17
Bananarama 17
Banshee 17
Beaufort Connection 17
beer glasses 145, 148, (149)
Bee Sting (mocktail) 17
Beetlejuice (shooter) 18
Bellini 18
Better than Sex 18
Between the Sheets 18
Bitter Apples (mocktail) 18
Bitter Lime (mocktail) 18

Black and Tan 170
Black and Tan (mocktail) 19
Black Jellybean, see Jellybean (note).
Black Magic 19
Black Nipple (shooter) 19
Black Nuts, No 1 19
Black Nuts, No 2 (shooter) 19
Black Russian, No 1 20
Black Russian, No 2 (short) 20
Black Russian, No 3 (long) 20
Black Velvet (champagne cocktail) 20
Black Widow (shooter) 20
blend (mixing term) 128
blenders 140, (141)
Blood Alcohol Concentration (B.A.C.) 163,
    165
Bloodbath (shooter) 20
Bloody Lovely 22
Bloody Mary (21), 22, (116)
Bloody Mary mix 127
Blow Job (shooter) 22
Blueberry Delight 22
Blue Hawaii 22
Blue Lady 22
Blue Lagoon, No 1 23
Blue Lagoon, No 2 23
Blue Negligée 23
Boilermaker 23
Bosom Caresser 23
Boston shakers 136, (137)
bottle openers 139
Brandy Alexander, No 1 23
Brandy Alexander, No 2 24, (25), (111)
brandy balloon (glass) 152
Brandy Crusta (2), 24, (120)
Brandy Egg-nog 24
Brandy, Lime and Soda 24
Brandy Sour, see Whiskey Sour (note).
Bronx 26
Brown Cow 26
Brown Cow, Sober (mocktail) 88
Bubble Gum 26
Buck's Fizz (champagne cocktail) 26
Buck's Fizzer (mocktail) 26
build (mixing term) 128
Bullshot 26
Bush Oyster, see Prairie Oyster (note).

Additional Recipes

NAME

INGREDIENTS

METHOD

GARNISH

GLASS

NAME

INGREDIENTS

METHOD

GARNISH

GLASS

NAME

INGREDIENTS

METHOD

GARNISH

GLASS

NAME

INGREDIENTS

METHOD

GARNISH

GLASS

NAME

INGREDIENTS

METHOD

GARNISH

GLASS

NAME

INGREDIENTS

METHOD

GARNISH

GLASS

NAME

INGREDIENTS

METHOD

GARNISH

GLASS

NAME

INGREDIENTS

METHOD

GARNISH

GLASS

NAME

INGREDIENTS

METHOD

GARNISH

GLASS

NAME

INGREDIENTS

METHOD

GARNISH

GLASS

NAME

INGREDIENTS

METHOD

GARNISH

GLASS

NAME

INGREDIENTS

METHOD

GARNISH

GLASS

NAME

INGREDIENTS

METHOD

GARNISH

GLASS

NAME

INGREDIENTS

METHOD

GARNISH

GLASS